James M. Le Moine

Tourist's Note-Book

James M. Le Moine

Tourist's Note-Book

ISBN/EAN: 9783337194635

Printed in Europe, USA, Canada, Australia, Japan

Cover: Foto ©Andreas Hilbeck / pixelio.de

More available books at **www.hansebooks.com**

THE

TOURIST'S

NOTE-BOOK

BY

J. M. LeMOINE,

AUTHOR OF

QUEBEC PAST & PRESENT.

SECOND EDITION.

QUEBEC:
F. X. GARANT & Co., EDITORS,
Fabrique street, Upper Town.

1876

CITY OF QUEBEC.

TO

Hon. W. C. HOWELLS,

CONSUL FOR THE UNITED STATES AT QUEBEC

—

These notes are inscribed in remembrance of the unceasing interest he has taken in the social and literary welfare of the citizens of Quebec,

By

The Author.

Spencer Grange,
    Dominion Day 1876.

INTRODUCTION.

The favor with which the first edition of this little book was received, has induced the writer to issue a second, in a more extended and as he hopes, a more useful form. It is unnecessary to observe that these desultory notes are not intended to take the place of a Guide-Book. Tourists seeking for thorough information on Quebec, are referred to the several Guide Books in circulation; those curious of studying its annals, will find them comprehensively set fourth in QUEBEC PAST AND PRESENT, just issued from the press: an illustrated volume of nearly 500 pages, to be had at any city book store.

It has been deemed useful to the cause of city improvements, to re-publish here, the excellent paper, contributed last winter, by Alex. J. Russell Esq., of Ottawa, in the *Ottawa Times*, on the Plans of City embellishment, suggested by the Earl of Dufferin.

J. M. LeMOINE.

SPENCER GRANGE,
    Dominion Day, 1876.

ST. LOUIS GATE.
Built 1693—Razed 1871.

QUEBEC,

AS SEEN BY AMERICAN, ENGLISH, FRENCH, AND CANADIAN WRITERS OF NOTE.

———

Quebec, founded by Samuel de Champlain, in 1608, has certainly much to recommend herself, by her monuments, her historical memories and her scenery, to the traveller — the scholar — the historian. The wintering of the venturesome Jacques Cartier on the banks of the St. Charles, in 1535-6, by its remoteness, is an incident of interest not only to Canadians, but also to every denizen of America. It takes one back to an era nearly coeval with the discovery of the continent by Columbus — much anterior to the foundation of Jamestown, in 1607 — anterior to that of St. Augustine in Florida, in 1592. Quebec has, then, a right to call herself an old, a very old. city of the west.

The colonization of Canada, or, as it was formerly called, New France, was undertaken by companies of French merchants engaged in the fur trade, close on whose steps followed a host of devoted missionaries, who found in the forests of this new and attractive country, ample scope for the exercise of their religious enthusiasm. It was at Quebec that these Christian heroes landed; from hence, they started for the forest primeval, the bearers of the olive branch of Christianity, of civilization.

A fatal mistake committed at the outset by the French commanders, in taking part in the Indian wars, more than once brought the incipient colony to the verge of ruin: during these periods, scores of devoted missionaries fell under the scalping knife or suffered incredible tortures, amongst the merciless savages whom they had come to reclaim. Indian massacres became so frequent, so appalling, that on several occasions the French thought of giving up the colony for ever. The rivalry between France and England, added to the hardships and dangers of the few hardy colonists established at Quebec. Its environs, the shores of its noble river, more than once became the battle-fields of European armies. These were periods of strife, happily gone by; we hope, forever.

In his "*Pioneers of France in the New World,*" the gifted Frs. Parkman mournfully reviews the vanished glories of old France in her former vast dominions, in America.

" The French dominion is a memory of the past; and when we evoke its departed shades, they rise upon us from their graves in strange romantic guise. Again their ghostly camp-fires seem to burn, and the fitful light is cast around on lord and vassal and black-robed priest, mingled with wild forms of savage warriors, knit in close fellowship on the same stern errand. A boundless vision grows upon us: an untamed continent

ST. JOHN'S GATE.
Built in 1693—Rebuilt in 1867.

vast wastes of forest verdure; mountains silent in primeval sleep; river, lake, and glimmering pool; wilderness oceans mingling with the sky. Such was the domain which France conquered for civilization. Plumed helmets gleamed in the shade of its forests; priestly vestments in its dens and fastnesses of ancient barbarism. Men steeped in antique learning, pale with the close breath of the cloister, here spent the noon and evening of their lives, ruled savage hordes with a mild, parental sway, and stood serene before the direst shapes of death. Men of a courtly nurture, heirs to the polish of a far-reaching ancestry, here, with their dauntless hardihood, put to shame the boldest sons of toil."

Of all this mighty empire of the past, Quebec was the undisputed capital, the fortress, the key-stone.

It would be a curious study to place in juxta position the impressions produced on Tourists by the view of Quebec and its environs—from Jacques Cartier, the discoverer of Canada, down to William Howard Russell.

Champlain, La Potherie, La Hontan, Le Beau, Du Creux (Creuxius), Peter Kalm, Knox, Silliman, Ampére, Mrs. Moodie, Anthony Trollope, Sala, Thoreau, Henry Ward Beecher, have all left their impressions of the rocky citadel.

"The scenic beauty of Quebec has been the theme of general eulogy. The majestic appearance of Cape Diamond and the fortifications, the cupolas and minarets, like those of an eastern city, blazing and sparkling in the sun, the loveliness of the panorama, the noble basin, like a sheet of purest silver, in which might ride with safety a hundred sail of the line, the graceful meandering of the river St. Charles, the numerous village spires on either side of the St. Lawrence, the fertile fields dotted with innumerable cottages, the abode of a rich and moral peasantry,—the distant falls of Montmorency,—the park like scenery of Pointe Levi,—the beauteous Isle of Orleans,—and more distant still, the frowning Cape Tourmente, and the lofty range of purple mountains of the most pictu resque form, which, without exaggeration, is scarcely to be surpassed in any part of the world." (Hawkins.)

" Quebec recalls Angoulême to my mind : in the upper city, stairways, narrow streets, ancient houses on the verge of the cliff; in the lower city, the new fortunes, commerce, workmen ;—in both, many shops and much activity. "(M. Sand.)

"Take mountain and plain, sinuous river, and broad, tranquil waters, stately ship and tiny boat, gentle hill and shady valley, bold headland and rich, fruitful fields, frowning battlement and cheerful villa, glittering dome and rural spire, flowery garden and sombre forest,—group them all into the choicest picture of ideal beauty your fancy can create ; arch it over with a cloudless sky, light it up with a radiant sun, and lest the sheen should be too dazzling, hang a veil of lighted haze over all, to soften the lines and perfect the repose,—you will then have seen Quebec on this September morning. " '(Eliot Warburton.)

HOPE GATE.
Built in 1786—Razed in 1871.

"I rubbed my eyes to be sure I was in the nineteenth century, and was not entering one of those portals which sometimes adorn the frontispiece of old black letter volumes. I thought it would be a good place to read Froissart's Chronicles. It was such a reminescence of the Middle Ages as Scott's Novels.

"Too much has not been said about the scenery of Quebec. The fortifications of Cap Diamond are omnipresent. You travel 10, 20, 30 miles, up or down the river's banks, you ramble 15 miles among the hills on either side, and then, when you have long since forgotten them, perchance slept on them by the way, at a turn of the road or of your body, then they are still with their geometry against the sky......

"No wonder if Jacques Cartier's pilot exclaimed in Norman-French *Que bec!* (" What a peak !)" when he saw this cape, as some suppose. Every modern traveller uses a similar expression......

"The view from Cape Diamond has been compared by European travellers with the most remarkable views of a similar kind in Europe, such as from Edinburgh Castle, Gibraltar, Cintra, and others and preferred by many. A main peculiarity in this, compared with other views which I have beheld, is that it is from the ramparts of a fortified city, and not from a solitary and majestic river cape alone that this view is obtained...I still remember the harbor far beneath me, sparkling like silver in the sun,—the answering headlands of Pointe Levi on the S. E.,—the frowning Cape Tourmente abrupty bounding the seaward view in the N. E.—the villages of Lorette and Charlesbourg on the North.—and farther West, the distant ValCaltier, sparkling with white cottages, hardly removed by distance through the clear air,—not to mention a few blue mountains along the horizon in that direction. You look out from the ramparts of the citadel beyond the frontiers of civilization. Yonder small group of hills, according to the guide-book, forms the portals of the wilds which are trodden only by the feet of the Indian hunters as far as Hudson's Bay."(Thoreau.)

Mrs. Moodie (Susannah Strickland), in her sketches of Canadian life, graphically delineates her trip from Grosse Isle to Quebec, and the appearance of the city itself from he river:

" On the 22nd of September (1832), the anchor was weighed, and we bade a long farewell to Grosse Isle. As our vessel struck into mid-channel, I cast a last lingering look at the beautiful shores we were leaving. Cradled in the arms of the St. Lawrence, and basking in the bright rays of the morning sun, the island and its sister group looked like a second Eden just emerged from the waters of chaos. The day was warm, and the cloudless heavens of that peculiar azure tint which gives to the Canadian skies and waters a brilliancy unknown in more northern latitudes. The air was pure and elastic; the sun shone out with uncommon spendour, lighting up the changing woods with a rich mellow colouring, composed of a thousand brilliant and vivid dyes. The mighty river rolled flashing and sparkling onward, impelled by a strong breeze that tipped its short rolling surges with a crest of snowy foam.

PALACE GATE.
Built 1750—Rebuilt 1831—Razed 1871.

" Never shall I forget that short voyage from Grosse Isle to Quebec. What wonderful combinations of beauty and grandeur and power, at every winding of that noble river!

" Every perception of my mind became absorbed into the one sense of seeing, when, upon rounding Point Levi, we cast anchor before Quebec. What a scene! Can the world produce another? Edinburgh had been the *beau ideal* to me of all that was beautiful in nature — a vision of the Northern Highlands had haunted my dreams across the Atlantic; but all these past recollections faded before the *present* of Quebec. Nature has ransacked all our grandest elements to form this astonishing panorama. There, frowns the cloud-capped mountain, and below, the cataract foams and thunders; woods and rock and river combine to lend their aid in making the picture perfect, and worthy of its Divine originator. The precipitous bank upon which the city lies piled, reflected in the still, deep waters at its base, greatly enhance the romantic beauty of the situation. The mellow and serene glow of the autumn day harmonized so perfectly with the solemn grandeur of the scene around me, and sank so silently and deeply into my soul, that my spirit fell prostrate before it, and I melted involuntarily into tears."

Such the poetic visions which were awakened in the poetic mind of the brilliant author of " *Roughing it, in the Bush.*"

A distinguihed French *littérateur*, fresh from the

sunny banks of the Seine, thus discourses anent the ancient capital ; we translate :

" Few cities," says M. Marmier, (1) " offer as many striking contrasts as Quebec, a fortress and a commercial city together, built upon the summit of a rock as the nest of an eagle, while her vessels are everywhere wrinkling the face of the ocean ; an American city inhabited by French colonists, governed by England, and garrisoned with Scotch regiments ; (2) a city of the middle ages by most of its ancient institutions while it is submitted to all the combinations of modern constitutional government ; an European city by its civilization and its habits of refinement, and still close by, the remnants of the Indian tribes and the barren mountains of the north ; a city with about the same latitude as Paris, while successively combining the torrid climate of southern regions with the severities of an hyperborean winter ; a city at the same time Catholic and Protestant, where the labours of our (French) missions are still uninterrupted alongside of the undertakings of the Bible Society, and where the Jesuits driven out of our own country (France) find a place of refuge under the ægis of British Puritanism !"

An American tourist thus epitomises the sights :

" As the seat of French power in America until 1759, the great fortress of English rule in British America, and the key of the St. Lawrence, Quebec must possess

---

(1) *Lettres sur l'Amérique :* X. Marmier. Paris, 1869.
(2) The Highlanders—78th, 79th, and 93rd.

PRESCOTT GATE.
Built in 1797—Razed in 1871.

interest of no ordinary character for well-informed tourists. To the traveller, there are innumerable points and items vastly interesting and curious :—the citadel and forts of Cape Diamond, with their impregnable ramparts that rival Gibraltar in strength and endurance against siege; the old walls of the city and their gates, each of which has its legend of war and bloody assault and repulse; the plains of Abraham, every foot of which is commemorated with blood and battle; Wolfe's monument, where the gallant and brave soldier died with a shout of victory on his lips; the Martello towers, with their subterranean communications with the citadel; the antique churches, paintings, and all her paraphernalia, treasures, and curiosities that are religiously preserved therein; the falls of Montmorenci; the natural steps; Montcalm's house, and a thousand other relics of the mysterious past that has hallowed these with all the mystic interest that attaches to antiquity, great deeds, and beautiful memories. To see all these, a tourist requires at least two days' time; and surely no one who pretends to be a traveller, in these days of rapid transit, will fail to visit Quebec, the best city, the most hospitable place, and richer in its wealth of rare sights and grand old memorials, French peculiarities and English oddities, than any other city on this broad continent."

In the rosy days of his budding fame, the gifted Henry Ward Beecher discourses as follows, of the Rock City.

"Curious old Quebec!—of all the cities on the continent of America, the quaintest. * * * It is a populated cliff. It is a mighty rock, scarped and graded, and made to hold houses and castles which, by a proper natural law, ought to slide off from its back, like an ungirded load from a camel's back. But they stick. At the foot of the rocks, the space of several streets in width has been stolen from the river. * * * We landed. * * * *

"Away we went, climbing the steep streets at a canter with little horses hardly bigger than flies, with an aptitude for climbing perpendicular walls. It was strange to enter a walled city through low and gloomy gates, on this continent of America. Here was a small bit of mediæval Europe perched upon a rock, and dried for keeping, in this north-east corner of America, a curiosity that has not its equal, in its kind, on this side of the ocean. * * * * *

"We rode about as if we were in a picture-book, turning over a new leaf at each street! * * * * The place should always be kept old. Let people go somewhere else for modern improvements. It is a shame, when Quebec placed herself far out of the way, up in the very neighbourhood of Hudson's Bay, that it should be hunted and harassed with new-fangled notions, and all the charming inconveniences and irregularities that narrow and tortuous streets, that so delight a traveller's eyes, should be altered to suit the fantastic notions of modern people. * * *

"Our stay in Quebec was too short by far. But it was long enough to make it certain that we shall come back again. A summer in Canada would form one of the most delightful holidays that we can imagine. We mean to prove our sincerity by our conduct. And then, if it is not all that our imagination promises, we will write again and confess."1

Professor Benjamin Silliman discourses thus:

"A seat of ancient dominion—now hoary with the lapse of more than two centuries—formerly the seat of a French empire in the west—lost and won by the blood of gallant armies, and of illustrious commanders—throned on a rock, and defended by all the proud defiance of war! Who could approach such a city without emotion? Who in Canada has not longed to cast his eyes on the water-girt rocks and towers of Quebec?"—(SILLIMAN's *Tour in Canada*, 1819.

Let us complete this mosaic of descriptions and literary gems, borrowed from English, French, and American writers, by a sparkling *tableau* of the historic memories of Quebec, traced by a French Canadian *littérateur* of note: Honb. P. J. O. Chauveau.

"History is everywhere—around us beneath us; from the depths of yonder valleys, from the top of that mountain, history rises up and presents itself to to our notice, exclaiming: 'Behold me!'

"Beneath us, among the capricious meanders of the River St. Charles, the Cahir-Coubat of Jacques-Cartier, is the very place where he first planted the cross and held his first conference with the *Seigneur Donaconna*. Here, very near to us, beneath a venerable elm tree, which, with much regret, we saw cut

---

(1) New-York *Ledger*.

down, tradition states that Champlain first raised his tent. From the very spot on which we now stand, Count de Frontenac returned to Admiral Phipps that proud answer, as he said, *from the mouth of his cannon*, which will always remain recorded by history. Under these ramparts are spread the plains on which fell Wolfe and Montcalm, and where, in the following year, the Chevalier de Lévis and General Murray fought that other battle, in memory of which the citizens of Quebec are erecting (in 1854) a monument. Before us, on the heights of Beauport, the souvenirs of battles not less heroic, recall to our remembrance the names of Longueuil, St. Hélène, and Juchereau Duchesnay. Below us, at the foot of that tower on which floats the British flag, Montgomery and his soldiers all fell, swept by the grape-shot of a single gun pointed by a Canadian artilleryman.

"On the other hand, under that projecting rock, now crowned with the guns of old England, the intrepid Dambourgès, sword in hand, drove Arnold and his men from the houses in which they had established themselves. History is then everywhere around us. She rises as well from these ramparts, replete with daring deeds, as from those illustrious plains equally celebrated for feats of arms, and she again exclaims: 'Here I am!'"

SEMINAIRE DES MISSIONS ETRANGERES.
1663.

Hints to Tourists visiting Quebec.

There is a magnificent line of steamers leaving Montreal every evening, at 7 P. M., and reaching Quebec at 6 A. M., In additition to these floating palaces, equal to those on the Hudson, the Grand Trunk Railway Company run two trains per day to Quebec from Montreal: there is also the Massawappi and Passumpsic Railway.

Living is comparatively cheap, and hotel accommodation is as good as any Canadian city can furnish. There are at Quebec several dozen of minor hotels, and some extensive ones, such as Noonan's, Henchey's, the Mountain Hill House and Blanchard's Hotels, without counting the large Victoria Hotel at South Quebec. Three large hotels—the St. Louis Hotel, the Clarendon and the ALBION, kept on the American principle—have, of course, from their size, the first claim on the traveller's attention; and the rush of visitors at these hotels during the summer months sufficiently testifies to the comfort and civility, which await the traveller.

The city and environs abound in drives varying from five to thirty miles, in addition to being on the direct line of travel to the far-famed Saguenay,

---

(1) For full particulars, see " QUEBEC PAST AND PRESENT."

Murray Bay, Kamouraska, Cacouna, Rimouski, Métis, Gaspé, and other noted watering places.

Quebec can minister abundantly to the tastes of those who like to ride, drive, fish, or shoot.

Let us see what the city contains :—First, the St. Louis Château : the corner stone of the wing still existing was laid on 5th May 1784 by Governor Haldimand, to enlarge the *old* Chateau (burnt down in January, 1834): this mouldering pile, now used as the Normal School, is all that remains of the stately edifice of old, overhanging and facing the Cul-de-Sac, where the lordly Count de Frontenac held his quasi regal court in 1691 ; next, the Laval University, founded in 1854, conferring degrees under its royal charter. The course of studies is similar to that of the celebrated European University of Louvain ; then, there is the Quebec Seminary, erected by Bishop Laval, a Montmorency, in 1663 ; the Ursuline Convent, founded in 1639 by Madame de la Peltrie ; this nunnery, with the Basilica, which was built in 1646, contains many valuable paintings, which left France about 1817 ; the General Hospital, founded in 1693 by Monseigneur de St. Vallier; in 1759, it was the chief hospital for the wounded and dying during the memorable battle of the 13th September—Arnold and his continentals found protection against the rigors of a Canadian winter behind its walls in 1775-6 ; the *Hotel-Dieu* nunnery, close to Palace Gate, dating more than two hundred years back.

As to the views to be obtained from Durham Terrace, the Glacis and the Citadel, they are unique in grandeur ; each street has its own familiar vista of the surrounding country. It is verily, as Henry Ward Beecher well expresses it, " like turning over the leaves of a picture-book."

A city crowning the summit of a lofty cape must necessarily be arduous of access; and when it is remembered how irregular is the *plateau* on which it stands, having yet for thoroughfares the identical Indian paths of Stadacona, or the narrow avenues and approaches of its first settlers in 1608, it would be vain to hope for regularity, breadth, and beauty, in streets such as many modern cities can glory in. It is yet in its leading features, a city of the 17th century. —a quaint, curious, drowsy, but healthy location for human beings ; a cheap place of abode ; if you like, a crenelated fort, with loop-holes, grim-looking old guns, embrasures, pyramids of shot and shell; such the spectacle high up in the skies, in the airy locality called the Upper Town. Some hundred feet below, it exhibits a crowded mart of commerce, with vast beaches, where rafts of timber innumerable rest in safety, a few perches from where a whole fleet of *Great Easterns* might ride secure, on the waters of the famed river. The two main roads outside the city, the St. Foye and St. Lewis Roads, are lined with the country seats of successful Quebec merchants, judges, professional men, retired English officers, &c.

On his way from the St. Louis Hotel, St. Louis street,

the tourist notices, a few steps westward, first the Music Hall, next the antiquated one-story house where Brigadier General Richard Montgomery was laid out after being found in his snowy shroud at Près-de-Ville, on the 31st December, 1775. This decayed old dwelling is but one story high. In 1775, it belonged to one Gobert, a cooper; and Brigadr.-General Montgomery's remains, after having been identified by Mrs. Miles Prentice, by a scar on his face, were deposited there, and removed on the 4th January, 1776 to be buried in the gorge of the bastion at Louis Gate. Mr. L. G. Baillairgé, advocate, the present owner of this house, has commemorated this incident by an inscription on it, visible to every beholder. Nor has tradition failed to surround this antiquated rookery with her mystic halo. More than one Jehu has poured into the willing ear of tourists, the sorrowful tale of the great soldier's burial and pointed out the hole cut through the partition of the small room, in order to stretch to their full length the long legs of the illustrious dead hero, when he was laid out. It is to be hoped some enthusiastic Irish antiquary will yet spring up in the old city, who will be able to restore and set to music, the wail which echoed through the building, at Montgomery's wake; no decent Hibernian would in those days have been allowed to die without a wake.

After passing the Drill-Shed, the Female Orphan Asylum, the Ladies' Protestant Home, facing St. Bridget's Asylum, and adjoining the area which the Quebec Seminary intended to lay out as a Botanical Garden, the

BIRD'S EYE VIEW OF URSULINES CONVENT.

Jehu, amidst miraculous details of the great battle, soon lands his passenger on the Plains of Abraham, close to the little monument which marks the spot where James Wolfe, the British hero, expired. To the east, is the well from which water was procured to moisten his parched lips. A few minutes more brings the tourist to M. Price's villa, Wolfe-field, where may be seen the pricipitous path up the St. Denis burn, by which the Highlanders and British soldiers gained a footing above, on the 13th September, 1759, and met in battle array to win a victory destined to revolutionize the new world. The British, were piloted in their ascent of the St. Lawrence by a French prisoner brought with them from England—Denis de Vitré, formerly a Quebecer of distinction. Their landing place at Sillery was selected by Major Robert Stobo, who had, in May, 1759, escaped from a French prison in Quebec, and joined his countrymen, the English, at Louisbourg, from whence, he took ship again to meet Saunders' fleet at Quebec. The tourist next drives past Thornhill, Sir Francis Hincks' old home, when Premier to Lord Elgin ; opposite, appear the leafy glades of Spencer Wood, so grateful a summer retreat, that my Lord used to say, " There he not only loved to live, but would like to rest his bones." Next comes Spencer Grange, the seat of J. M. LeMoine, Esq. ; then, Woodfield, the homestead of the Hon. Wm. Sheppard, in 1847, now of Messrs. John L. and Jas. Gibb. The eye next dwells on the rustic Church of St. Michael, embowered in evergreens ; close to which looms out, at *Sous les Bois*, the stately convent of *Jesus-Marie ;* then, you see villas innumerable—

that is, if you enter beyond the secluded portals of Benmore, Col. Rhodes' country seat; Benmore is well worthy of a call, where it only to procure a *bouquet*. This is not merely the Eden of roses, Col. Rhodes has combined the farm with the garden. His underground rhubarb and mushroom cellars, his boundless asparagus beds and strawberry plantations, are a source of profit to himself and credit to Quebec. Next come Clermont, Beauvoir, Kilmarnock, Cataraqui, Kilgraston, Kirk-Ella, Meadow Bank, &c.,until, after a nine-miles'drive, Redclyffe closes the rural landscape—Redclyffe, on the top of Cap Rouge promontory. There, many indications yet mark the spot where Roberval's ephemeral colony wintered as far back as 1542. You can now, if you like, return to the city by the same route, or select the St. Foye Road, skirting the classic heights where General Murray, six months after the first battle of the Plains, lost the second, on the 28th April, 1760; the St. Foye Church was then occupied by the British soldiers. Your gaze next rests on Holland House, Montgomery's headquarters in 1775, behind which is Holland Tree, overshadowing, as of yore, the grave of the Hollands. (1)

The view, from the St. Foye road, of the meandering St. Charles below, especially during the high tides, is something to be remembered. The tourist shortly after detects the iron pillar, surmounted by a bronze statue of Bellona, presented in 1855 by Prince Napoleon Bonaparte—intended to commemorate the fierce

---

(1) For account of the duel, which laid low one of the Hollands, see *Maple Leaves* for 1863. The tree however has lately been destroyed by a storm.

MONUMENT OF STE. FOYE.
1760.

struggle of 28th April, 1760. In close vicinity, appear the bright *parterres* or umbrageous groves of *Bellevue*, Hamwood, Bijou, Westfield, *Sans-Bruit*, and the narrow gothic arches of the Finlay Asylum; soon the traveller re-enters by St. John's suburbs, with the broad basin of the St. Charles and the pretty Island of Orleans staring him in the face. Let him drive down next to see the Montmorency Falls and the little room which the Duke of Kent, Queen Victoria's father occupied there in 1793. A trip to the Island of Orleans by the ferry will also repay trouble; half an hour of brisk steaming will do it. The Island contains passable hotel accommodation. Let him cross then to St. Joseph, Lévi, in the ferry steamer, and go and behold the most complete, the most formidable, as to plan, the most modern earthworks in the world, making one forget those of Antwerp. They are capable containing three regiments of soldiers. At a point to the north-east of the lower fort, a plunging fire from above can be brought to bear, which would sink the most invulnerable iron clad in the world.

STADACONA DEPICTA.

BY THE OLDEST INHABITANT.

" Be it so, my young friend : a quiet ramble we shall have, outside the old city gates. Lend an attentive

---

(1) The following sketch being an extract from a work in preparation for the press, will cover a deal of ground not included in what proceeds, Some of the best liked pages of the *Maples Leaves*, I owe to my kind old friend Mr. Sheppard, who died in 1867, leaving behind him the reputation of an elegant scholar and of an honest man. He is supposed here to speak by the mouth of the " oldest inhabitant."

ear to the oft told tales of a garrulous old fellow; Since I left the green banks of Woodfield, in 1847, for my cottage-home, at Fairymead, gigantic strides have been made towards unveiling the early history of our country. Under the pen of Garneau, Ferland, Holmes, Miles, Faribault and others, the annals of this portion of Canada have stalked forth in radiant majesty; Canada is now known far and wide. Still I may yet, perchance, contribute a few tiles to the mosaïc of the local history of my native town.

Let us examine the surroundings of that strange "Old Curiosity Shop," so quaintly sketched by Henry Ward Beecher.

We will first tread over the classic ground to the west of the city, from St. Louis gate, to Cap Rouge.

One of the earliest incidents, I can remember, was a ball given about 1793, by Mr. Lymburner, (Adam, I think, was his name), at his mansion in St. Peter Street, when the Duke of Kent, our Queen's father attended. This popular sprig of royalty, was then known to our French Canadian fellow citizens, as "Le Prince Edouard." I think I see his burly form reviewing the troops in the *Place d'Armes*, in front of the *Old Chateau*. The incident clings to my memory, from the fact that the soldier who beat the big drum in the band, was a negro. Adam Lymburner, His Grace's entertainer, was a man of note and ability; he was selected, and deputed to England in 1791, to make representations to the Home Government, on Provincial matters. You can read his able discourse in

HOPITAL-GENERAL CONVENT.

the *Canadian Review*, published at Montreal in 1826. This locality has also become historical ground. Here Benedict Arnold and his men, were defeated by Governor Guy Carleton's intrepid followers, on the 31st December, 1775 : here, MajorNairn and Dambourges won imperishable fame by the pluck they showed in repelling the invaders of their country whilst the double traitor Arnold, wounded in the knee, was carried to the General Hospital. No doubt, learned old Lymburner exhibited to Royal Edward, from the drawing-room windows, the spot adjoining, (in rear of W. D. Campbell's notarial office,) where eighteen years previous, King George's Canadian lieges, by their bravery, added new lustre to the British Arms. By the by, we have come through the *Port St. Louis* without saluting, as we glided past the modest, very modest little house (now a pastry cook's shop, formerly the cooperage of Gobert, No. 38 St. Louis Street,) where, a brave but unlucky Commander, was lying stiff and cold, one New Year's day last century. Alas ! poor Richard Montgomery,— (1) Wolfe's companion in arms, in 1759. Had promotion gone on smoothly and justly in your old *corps*, the 17th Foot, you would not have sold out, and levied war against

(1) Brigadier Richard Montgomery, who fell at Quebec in 1775 was born in Ireland in 1735,—studied at Trinity College Dublin, was commissionned as Ensign in the 17th Foot on 21st aug. 1750—served under Wolfe at Louisbourg, in 1758—was promoted to a Lieutenancy 10th ang. 1758. Served under Amherst in 1756, on Lake Champlain—under Col. Haviland at the reduction of Montreal in 1760—Subsequently went to the West Indies—left New-York for England in 1767—sold out in 1772 and came to America in 1773.

Britain, your country, and when my friend, Deputy Commissary General Thompson, hands me your trusty old rapier, (1) and I reflect what nature had made you, I felt as if I could weep, on viewing your untimely end, at Près-de-Ville, on the 31st December, 1775.

Within a stone's throw from Gobert's, where Montgomery was "waked," is the late Chief Justice Jonathan Sewell's (2) Mansion, facing the Esplanade.

On emerging from St. Louis gate, the first object which attracts the eye, is the straggling form of the Skating Rink ; opposite, stands or rather *leans* on props, a structure still more unsightly,—the Racket Court, much frequented by Lord Monck, when in Quebec. Adjoining, you notice, the old home of the Prentices, in 1791,—Bandon Lodge, (3) once the abode of Sandy Simpson (4) whose cat.-o-nine tails, has left lively memories in Wolfe's army — Did the beauteous damsel about whom Horatio, Lord Nelson,

---

(1) This famous Escalibur has been recently deposited for safe keeping in the museum of the *Literary and Historical* Society at Quebec, by its present owner James Thompson Harrower, Esquire.

(2) It now contains the Executive Council Room, and Lieut.-Governor's town Office.

(3) Now a Boarding House, kept by Mrs. Torrance.

(4) SAUNDERS SIMPSON.—" He was Provost Marshal in Wolfe's army, at the affairs of Louisbourg, Quebec and Montreal, and cousin of my Father's. He resided in that house the nearest to Saint Louis Gate, outside, which has not undergone any external alteration since I was a boy."—*From Diary of Deputy Commissary General Jas. Thompson.*

JACQUES-CARTIER

raved in 1782, when, as Commander of the *Albemarle*, sloop of war, he was philandering in Quebec, live here? This is more than I can say. Close by, looms out the long, tea, caddy looking building, built by the Sandfield McDonald Government in 1862,—the Volunteer Drill Shed. Its length, if not beauty, attracts notice. " Ferguson's house," next to it, noted by Professor Silliman in his " Tour between Hartford and Quebec in 1819," is now difficult to recognize; its present owner, A. Joseph, Esq., has added so to it. Another land-mark of the past deserves notice—the ex-Commander of the Force's lofty Quarters—from its angular eaves and forlorn aspect, it generally goes by the name of " Bleak House." I cannot say whether it ever was haunted, but it ought to have been. We are now in the *Grande Allée*—the forest avenue, which two hundred years ago led to Sillery Wood. On turning and looking back as you approach this singular house, you have an excellent view of the Citadel, and of the old French works, which extend beyond it, to the extremity of the Cape, overlooking l'*Anse des Mères*. A little beyond the Commandant's house, at the top of what is generally known as Perrault's Hill, stands the Perrault homestead, dating back to 1820, l'Asyle *Champêtre*,—now handsomely renovated and owned by Henry Dinning, Esq. The adjoining range of heights, at present occupied by the Martello Towers, is known as the *Buttes-à-Nepveu*. " It was here, that Murray took his stand on the morning of April 28th, 1760, to resist the advance of Levis, and here commenced the hardest fought—the bloodiest action of the war, which terminated in the defeat of Murray, and his retreat within the City. The Martello towers are bombproof, they are three in number, and form a chain of forts extending along the ridge from the St. Lawrence to the River St. Charles. The fact that this ridge commanded the City, unfortunately induced Murray to leave it, and attempt to fortify the heights in which he was only partially successful owing to the frost being still in the ground.

The British Government were made aware of the fact, and seeing that from the improved artillery, the City was now fully commanded from the heights which are about seven hundred yards distant, decided to build the Towers. Arrangements were accordingly made by Col. Brock, then commanding the troops in Canada. In 1806, the necessary materials were collected, and in the following year, their construction commenced. They were not however completed till 1812. The original estimate for the four was £8,000, but before completion the Imperial government had expended nearly £12,000. They are not all of the same size, but like all Martello Towers, they are circular and bomb-proof. The exposed sides are *thirteen* feet thick and gradually diminish like the horns of the crescent moon, to *seven* feet in the centre of the side next the City walls. The first or lower story contains, tanks, storerooms and magazine: the second, has cells for the garrison, with port-holes for two guns. On the top, there used to be one 68 pounder carronade, two 24, and two 9 pounders."

A party of Arnold's soldiers ascended these heights in November, 1775, and advanced quite close to the City walls, shouting defiance at the little garrison A few shots, soon dispersed the invaders, who retraced their steps to Wolfe's Cove. On the *Buttes-à-Nepveu*, the great criminals were formerly executed. Here, La Corriveau the St. Vallier Lafarge, met her deserved fate in 1763, after being tried by one of Governor Murray's Court Martials for murdering her husband. After death, she was hung in chains, or rather in a solid iron cage, at the fork of four roads, at Levi, close to the spot where the Temperance monument has since been built. The loathsome form of the murderess caused more than one shudder amongst the peaceable peasantry of Levi, until some brave young men, one dark night cut down the horrid cage, and hid it deep under ground, next to the cemetery at Levi, where close to a century afterwards, it was dug up and sold to Barnum's agent for his Museum.

Sergeant Jas. Thompson, records in his Diary, under date 18th Nov., 1782, another memorable execution :

"This day two fellows were executed for the murder and robbery of Capt. Stead, Commander of one of the Treasury Brigs, on the evening of the 31st Dec., 1779, between the Upper and the Lower Town. The criminals went through Port St. Louis, about 11 o'clock, at a slow and doleful pace, to the place where justice has allotted them to suffer the most ignominious death. It is astonishing to see what a crowd of people followed the tragic scene. Even our people on the works (Cape Diamond) prayed Capt. Twiss for leave to follow the hard-hearted crowd." It was this Capt. Twiss who subsequently furnished the plan and built a temporary citadel.

Eleven years later, in 1793, we have, recorded in history, another doleful procession of red coats, the Quebec Garrison, accompanying to the same place of execution, a mess-mate (Draper), a soldier of the 16th Fusileers, then commanded by the young Duke of Kent, who, after pronouncing the sentence of death, as Commander, over the trembling culprit kneeling on his coffin, as son and representative of the Sovereign, exercised the royal prerogative of mercy and pardoned poor Draper.

Look down the hill, to the south. There stands, with a few shrubs and trees in the foreground, the Military Home,—where infirm soldiers, their widows and children, could find a refuge.—It has recently been purchased and converted into the "Female Orphan Asylum." It forms the eastern boundary of a large expanse of verdure and trees, reaching the summit of the lot originally intended by the Seminary of Quebec, for a Botanical Garden.

Its western boundary is a road leading to the new District Jail,—a stone structure of great strength, surmounted with a diminutive tower, admirably adapted, one would imagine, for astronomical pursuits. From its glistening cupola, Commander Ashe's Provincial Observatory is visible to the east. A lofty red fence surrounding the western portion of this Tolbooth, might have been seen from the St. Louis Road. It invested the abode of crime with a sanguinary aspect. During the middle ages, when great criminals were occasionally flayed alive, this blood red circumvallation might have been mistaken for the bleaching hides of murderers, heretics, sorcerers and witches. It has ever, in my mind, been associated with a warning to erring humanity. Beware of the red Fence! (1)

I was forgetting to notice that substantial building, dating from 1855—the Ladies Home. The Protestant Ladies of Quebec, have here, at no small expense and trouble, raised a fitting monument, where the aged and infirm may find shelter, food and raiment. This, and the building opposite, St. Bridget's Asylum, with its fringe of trees and green plots, are decided ornaments to the *Grande Allée*.

The old burying ground of 1832, with all its ghastly memories of the Asiatic scourge, through the taste and liberality of our Irish brethren, has assumed quite an ornate, nay a respectable aspect. Near the angle of DeSalaberry Street, on the *Grande Allée*, may yet be seen one of the stones which serve to mark the western boundary of the city, to the west of the Lampson Mansion. On the adjoining domain, well named " Battlefield Cottage," formerly the property of Col. Charles Campbell, now owned by M.

---

(1) Since these lines were written, the red has disappeared under a coat of whiteish paint.

Conolly, Esq., was the historic well out of which a cup of water was obtained to moisten the parched lips of the dying hero, Wolfe, on the 13th Sept., 1759. The well was filled in a few years ago, but not before it was nigh being fatal to Col. Campbell's young son, — (Arch. Campbell, Esq., of Thornhill.) Its site is close to the western boundary fence, in the garden behind "Battlefield Cottage." Here we are at those immortal plains—the Hastings and Runnymede of the two races once arrayed in battle against one other.

Let us allow W. D. Howells, the brilliant writer of "Our Wedding Journey," to describe the incidents we have just glanced over :

"The fashionable suburban cottages and places of Quebec, are on the St. Louis Roard, leading northward to the old battle ground, and beyond it; but these, face chiefly towards the Rivers St. Lawrence and St. Charles, and lofty hedges and shrubbery hide them in an English seclusion from the highway; so that the visitor may uninterruptedly meditate whatever emotion he will for the scene of Wolfe's death, as he rides along. His loftiest emotion will want the noble height of that heroic soul, who must always stand forth in history a figure of beautiful and singular distinction, admirable alike for the sensibility and daring, the poetic pensiveness, and the martial ardor that mingled in him, and taxed his feeble frame with tasks greater than it could bear. The whole story of the capture of Quebec is full of romantic splendor

MONTCALM.

and pathos. Her fall was a triumph for the English-speaking race, and to us Americans, long scourged by the cruel Indian wars plotted within her walls, or sustained by her strength, such a blessing as was hailed with ringing bells and blazing bonfires throughout the Colonies; yet now, we cannot think without pity of the hopes extinguished and the labors brought to nought in her overthrow. That strange colony of priests and soldiers, of martyrs and heroes, of which she was the capital, willing to perish for an allegiance to which the mother country was indifferent, and fighting against the armies with which England was prepared to outnumber the whole Canadian population, is a magnificent spectacle; and Montcalm laying down his life to lose Quebec, is not less affecting than Wolfe dying to earn her. The heart opens towards the soldier who recited, on the eve of his costly victory, the " ' Elegy in a Country Churchyard,' which he would rather have written than beat the French to-morrow;" but it aches for the defeated general, who, hurt to death, answered when told how brief his time was, " So much the better; then I shall not live to see the surrender of Quebec."

In the City for which they perished, their fame has never been divided. The English have shown themselves very generous victors; perhaps nothing could be alleged against them, but that they were victors."

A trip to the Chandière Falls, nine miles distant, cannot be omitted,—no more than a drive to Lake St. Charles by Indian Lorette, and a *sail* in a birch bark canoe to the sounding shores of Echo Bay. Diverge to the east, and drive to Lake Beauport, to luxuriate on its red trout; but mind you stop, on your return, and take a caulker of Glenlivet or old Bourbon or Sillery Mousseux, on the banks of the trout stream, next to the Hermitage, at Charlesbourg. Step into the *Chateau;* sit down, like Volney amidst the ruins of Palmyra, and meditate on the romantic, though unhappy, fate of dark-eyed Caroline, Bigot's Rosamond, (1) some hundred years ago. You imagine you have seen everything; not so, my friend! Tell your driver to let you out, opposite Ringfield, on the Charlesbourg road, and, if at home, Mr. G. H. Parke, the obliging proprietor, will surely grant you leave to visit the extensive earthworks, behind his residence, raised by Montcalm in 1759—so appropriately called Ringfield. Hurry back to town in time to accept *that* invitation to dine at the Club; then spend the evening agreably at the Morrin College, in the cosy rooms of the *Literary and Historical Society*, and retire early, preparing yourself for the great compaign of the morrow. To the Lakes! To the Lakes! Here are a few of them: Lake Calvaire, at St. Augustin; Lake St. Joseph, *Lac à la Truite*, *Lac Philipe*, *Lac Jaune*, Snow Lake, *Lac Blanc*, *Lac Sud-ouest*, *Lac Vincent*, *Lac Thomas*, *Lac Claire*, Lake Mackenzie, Lake Sagamite, Lake Burns, Lake Bonnet—all within a few hours' drive from Quebec, with the exception of Snow Lake. It

---

(1) You can peruse Caroline's very pathetic tale in *Maple Leaves* for 1863.

RUINS OF INTENDANT'S PALACE.
Facing the St. Charles—Destroyed by English shells &c. 1759—Destroyed by the city guns in 1775-6 as affording a shelter to Arnold and Montgomery's soldiers.

is not uncommon to catch trout weighing from 12lbs. to 20lbs. in Lake St. Joseph and Snow Lake, during the winter months.

LORD NELSON.

The following note respecting the youthful amours of Lord Nelson, whilst at Quebec in 1782, were contributed by one of the "oldest inhabitants," To QUEBEC PAST AND PRESENT, but reached too late for insertion

MY RECOLLECTIONS OF THE PAST.

DEAR SIR,—I have much pleasure in acceeding to your request to send you a note of some circumstances connected with the city, in which seventy-one years of my life,— now verging towards eighty—have been spent. I am familiar with no part of Nelson's career, except what I heard from my mother's own lips respecting this brave man. My mother was gifted with a remarkable memory and recollected well having herself seen Captain Nelson, when in 1782, he commanded, at Quebec, the sloop-of-war Albemarle. "He was tall—stern of aspect and wore, as was then customary, the *queue* or pigtail" she often repeated, Hardy, afterward so famous, was, she used to say one of his lieutenants. Her idea of the Quebec young lady to whom he had taken such a violent fancy, was that her name was Woolsey—an aunt or elder sister, perhaps, of the late John W. Woolsey, Esq., President for some years of the Quebec Bank, who died in 1852, at a very advanced age. According to her, it was a Mr. Davidson, who prevented the imprudent marriage contemplated. (1)

As to the doings of the Press Gangs, in the Lower Town and suburbs I can speak from what I saw more than once. Impressing seamen lasted at Quebec from 1807, until after the battle of Waterloo. The terror these seafaring gentlemen created, was very great. I remember a fine young fellow who refused to surrender, being shot through the back with a holster pistol and dying of the wound : this was in 1810. I can name the following, as being seized by Press Gangs............ Soon ruses were resorted to, by the gay fellows who wandered after nightfall, in quest of amusement in the highways and by ways. Her Majesty's soldiers were of course, exempt of being impressed into the naval service: so, that our roving city youths would either borrow coats, or get some made, similar to the soldiers',—to elude the Press Gang. These ruses were however soon stopped ; the Press Gang, having secured the services of two city constables, Rosa and........, who could spot every city youth and point out the counterfeits.

R. URQUHART.

1 Who was Nelson's Quebec *inamorata* in 1782 ? This has puzzled many. Some said it was Miss Prentice ; others, her cousin Miss Simpson, a daughter of one of Wolfe's, Prevost-marshalls. *Adhuc sub judice lis est.*

OLD CHURCH—LOWER TOWN MARKET.
Notre Dame des Victoires, 1690 & 1711.

QUEBEC, AND EARL DUFFERIN'S PROPOSED REHABILITATION OF IT.

Such dusky grandeur clothed the height,
Where the huge castle holds its state,
And all the steep slope down,
Whose ridgy back heaves to the sky,
Piled deep and massy, close and high,
Mine own romantic town!
But Northward far, with purer blaze,
On Ochie mountains fell the rays,
And as each heathy top they kissed,
It gleamed a purple amethyst,
* * * * * * . * *

Fitz Eustace' heart felt closely pent,
As if to give his rapture vent,
The spur he to his charger lent,
And raised his bridle-hand,
And making demi-volte in air,
Cried, " Where's the coward that would not dare
To fight for such a land!"

" MARMION."

"In view of His Excellency's spirit-stirring proposal to restore, and further appropriately develope, the renowned historical aspect of the ancient metropolis of Canada—a little garrulous gossip may not be out of place about Quebec and "Auld Lang Syne." For, is it not the season for stories of olden time. We have classic authority for it:—does not Macaulay tell us that it was

" In the long nights of winter,
When the cold north winds blow,"

that the Romans told their stories of " the brave days of old.

Notwithstanding all that confederation of the Provinces and commercial developpement may have done, or in future do, for the elevation of other cities, Quebec is, and ever will be, to Canada what Rome is historically to Italy and Athens, to Greece. All patriotic and intelligent Canadians, alike of French and of British origin, must feel that it is to them an heirloom of common historic renown,—a powerful point of attraction, round which should gather sentiments of future common nationality. Were they too sordid to see it themselves, the literature and the general intelligence of the civilized world would tell them so.

Heroic history is a most costly product of any country: we should therefore preserve and make the most of what we have already got of it. Somewhat nearer, and northward, we have still greater, but less hospitable regions of which history is dumb, except as to some sea fights and forts capturing, on Hudson's Bay, unthought of now, owing to their insignificance in action and result.

In our old St. Lawrence and seaboard settlements, it is otherwise. Montreal and Three Rivers present many ancient interesting reminiscence; and the siege of extinct Louisburg was a great and tragic episode in the history of our country. Even the bombardment and destruction of La Petite Rochelle is of romantic interest, though so little known.

But the record of all these places weighs but little in the scale of history compared with that of Quebec, where the foundation of civilized society in Canada was first firmly laid, and the protracted duel between France and England for dominion on this continent was decisively fought to a conclusion destined to become the basis of our future Canadian nationality.

The idea, previously entertained, of destroying the walls of Quebec, and utilizing the ground occupied by them and their outworks for building purposes, was not only a mistake as regards the welfare of the city itself, but was also a contemplated wrong to the people of this country generally; who had reason to look upon it as a sad and unnecessary destruction, and an irreparable one, of very costly monuments of national history, unequalled on the continent; in which they also and their posterity had a right of property and common moral interest. Public feeling therefore warms to the proposed design of His Excellency for their preservation and picturesque development; and certainly posterity will thank him for his well judged and well imed intervention.

The construction of a continuous promenade around the entire circuit of the walls and outward base of the citadel, in the style proposed, would alone be a very great additional attraction to visitors, and source of enjoyment to the citizens. But the grand old historical idea of Quebec could never be fully realized, and the impression produced by it would be that of a magnificent, but headless, statue —if it be not created, as proposed, by a real and appropriate "Castle of St. Lewis," as a memorial of past and an insignia of present Vice-Regal dignity, and of the Imperial power it represents ; and nothing could tend more to realise such ideas, besides being beneficial in other ways, than the occasional presence of Her Majesty's representative at suitable seasons.

But some will say that it is all romantic, sentimental nonsense to set so much by national monuments and historical reminescences, now that we have logical common sense and political economy to guide us. But he must have studied the history of the world amiss, or not at all, who has not learned that after instinctive selfishness, sentiment has ever exercised an incomparably greater power therein than the doctrines of political economy ; and that the great difficulty is now, and ever has been, to get the world to be governed by sound logical common sense at all. Now, there's one half of society—the fair sex— God bless them—they are constitutionally illogical, and are all the better for it. They have sentiments always ready for their guidance, that are on the whole prettier, nicer, more benevolent and better, in a Christian point of view, than ours. And as to the power of such sentiment, there is Joan of Arc, that heroic saint and martyr, that should have been canonized long ago— was there an atom of political economy, logic, or what is called common sense in her project ?—Quite the reverse ; it was sheer sentiment, alone, that gave the overwhelming force, by which she liberated France, when trodden down, almost to political extinction, by foreign invasion. We see, on a great scale, the same world-turning force in the crusades. In the fall of the Greek Empire, we may judge what it might have done then. Had the Greeks of that time had the same sentiments of devoted patriotism and determined valour as their ancestors of Marathon and Thermopylæ, we may safely assume that they would have given the Turkish armies "to the raven and the kite." The sentiments that inspired the Scots at Bannockburn, and the Swiss at Morgarten, have done much, since, for both these nations (though small in numbers) and the people of them, as individuals, in maintaining their self respect. And what shall we say of the greater nations—England and France—what pecuniary sacrifices would they not make rather than fail to maintain that national honour which is based on their history? "Noblesse oblige;"—we who are the descendants or representatives of both these nationalities—is it not incumbent upon us to cherish such sentiments and transmit them to our posterity, who, with the aid of their influence, may be delivered from sinking into the ages of degradation, into which we see the descendants of eminent nations of old, have so often fallen.

With that view, we should appreciate the importance— as more advanced nations are now doing—of preserving and developing the characters of every monument and famous site, the reminiscenses of which are calculated to inspire and maintain such sentiments of historical renown and national honour; and, should recognize the suggesting of such works, so admirably designed for doing so as those now proposed, as appertaining to a more elevated and far seeing character of statesmanship than falls within the ordinary compass of political economy and finance.

Through the press, the proposed works have been fully and ably described and illustrated. The turrets and bridges will enhance the antique effect of the gates and walls, and the forming of a continuous promenade round the entire circuit of the ramparts and the outworks of the citadel will open the way to more imposing points of view, at present inaccessible or unfrequented, and complete a panorama of pictorial beauty and grandeur and historical interest combined, unequalled on this continent.

Without dwelling on the magnificent view from Durham Terrace, with which all are familiar, let us follow the proposed promenade through the Governor's Garden, past the monument to Wolfe and Montcalm, and up to the highest crest of the cliff from which the front wall of the citadel springs. From this point, inaccessible now, the view is much grander than from Durham Terrace; and the effect, from the nature of the position, very peculiar. Those who have climbed the long steps (since burned) that rose from the water edge to the citadel, will recollect the sensation it gave of clinging to the face of the cliff, like a fly to the wall; grim ramparts above you and grimmer rocks beneath, that plunge steeply down to the spot, far below, where the American General Montgomery was defeated and slain, in his daring attempt to surprise the upper town by way of Mountain street, a hundred years ago. Down below, the long, crowded line of shipping skirts the shore; and the dizzying effect of the elevation is increased by the impressive swiftness of the mighty river, which sweeps the crafts crossing it from their course, like corks in a mill race. Over and beyond the high cliffs opposite, and the picturesquely planted town of Levis that skirts and partly crests them, are the half-hidden fortifications on the highest summit; from which, in rich and varied scenery, the heights of Point Levis sweep down to the water edge, near the pretty, old fashioned Church of St. Joseph. Further beyond, with high swelling outline and wooded summit, as it recedes, the west end of the Island of Orleans projects upwards into the magnificent lake-like basin, into which the river expands below the city.

On the left, far beyond this noble expanse of water, the view is bounded on the north by the long array of the lofty, massive and generally dome-shaped summits of the Laurentian Mountains, the most majestic of which visible is Mountain Ste. Anne, about three thousand feet high. The eye follows them down the river, stretching far away, till, in the hazy distance of thirty miles, Cap Tourmente dips its vast disc of two thousand feet, abruptly down to the horizon.

The infinite continuity of dark forests, in which they are shrouded, adds a sombre grandeur to these very lofty hills. Their lower sloping uplands, and the lowlands beneath, that skirt the St. Lawrence, down through the parishes of Montmorenci, Ange Gardien, Chateau-Richer, Ste. Anne and St. Joachim, are exquisitely beautiful—lovely to distant view, but still more so to travel through. Adorned with occasional spires, and continous lines and groups of thickly clustered, bright dwellings; till pale and nebulous in the remotest distance, the keenest eye sight may trace the line of settlement sweeping abruptly up into the dim mountain region of the "Chemin du Cap."

Following the line of the proposed promenade, or rather the "corniche" along the top of the craggy steep, under the front wall of the citadel, and looking south westward up the river, the scene before us, though inferior in grandeur to that from which we have just turned, becomes more intensely interesting as we advance. The river, far beneath, expands to more than a mile and a half in width, forming the noble harbour of Quebec. The high cliffs continue along the south shore, till they break down near New Liverpool, towards the River Etchemin, which is seen foaming over the low but wide fall that bars its mouth, a little above which the St. Lawrence bends northward out of view behind the bold headland of Pointe a Pizeau, immediately above Wolfe's Cove. Behind the cliffs we see the high plateau, varied with fields and clumps and belts of wood, which extend till all is blended in the distance, in the great elevated plain of the St. Lawrence, which is seen stretching far away to where the blue summits of the great swelling hills of Megantic rise on the horizon.

To some of us, these remote blue summits recall pleasant days passed fifty years ago,

"A chasing the wild deer,
And a following the roe,"

roused before dawn of day from their lair, in the thickets of spruce and fir that crown these lofty hills; when the country behind them, back to the White Mountains of Maine, was utterly unknown and uninhabited, except by a few wandering Abenaquis (whose hereditary domain it was), and other Indians ; a vast solitude, whose silence was rarely broken by living sound, save that of the lonely owl by night, and the whippoorwill, and the bobolink by day.

Scanning the horizon, to the left of these high hills, we see a broad depression, where the sky line is unbroken by high summits, till they are again seen, swelling up in the townships of Cranbourne and Standon, far away southeastward, on the head waters of the River Etchemin ; behind the pretty looking settlements of Frampton, which are distinctly seen on the rising uplands thirty miles off. It was through that remote depression, following the River Chaudière, of which it is the valley, and down through the country before us, that Arnold led his toil-worn troops, in the fall of 1775 ; and crossing the St. Lawrence beneath us in canoes, landed at Wolfe's Cove, up there on the right, with five hundred men ; and ascending the heights took possession of St. Foye and the General Hospital, and held them till joined by General Montgomery, whom he succeeded in command in that unsuccessful seige.

Proceeding onwards, we reach the most interesting and impressive historical vestiges that Quebec has to show— the old French works. Their site is most commanding, and the surroundings magnificent. From the ruined stone work on the verge of a lofty and very prominent angle of the cliff which overhangs the strand three hundred and fifty feet below, a plunging view of most striking effect is obtained of Wolfe's Cove, crowded with shipping, and the track of Wolfe's daring ascent, with all that magnificent background, looking up the river already described. But it is the condition and expressive aspect of the grass-grown remains of the extensive ramparts and other works that speak so poetically of the past, that give the scene its intensely impressive and dreamy power. More than a century has passed since the smoke of the battle and the roar of the culverines have rolled away. For the long Sabbath of a hundred and twenty summers, the grass and the wild weeds have thriven upon them, undisturbed save by the bee and the butter-fly—the small birds that build their nests there—the solitary wanderer and the long bearded mumbling goats that grin grimly down on the mast heads and chimney tops far below ; but these vestiges of the past become only more venerable by increasing age and decay.

Turning from the cliffs that overhang the river, and following the route of the promenade round the base of the works that front the Plains of Abraham, a view of wider scope is obtained and of equally impressive character. The busy street, lined with shipping, is no longer seen. The massive works of the citadel, of great extent—silent, and grim with hidden strength, rise up behind us—and westward, in front, and a little beneath us, is the field of battle. The impression produced by the stern aspect of the citadel —the lonely old ramparts, sunk in decay—the desolate expanse in front of them with its martello towers, the historical recollections inspired by the battle field, give a character of solemnity to the scene which is enhanced by its magnificent extent.

Beyond the battle field is seen the plateau, on which it is situated, extending far, and richly diversified with villas, fields, lawns and woods. It sinks, on the left, to the great trench-like gorge in which flows the St. Lawrence, with its cliffs and magnificent distance ; and on the right, it falls to the picturesque valley of the St. Charles, bounded by the far reaching uplands and swelling hills, and remote, isolated mountains of the north.

There is no ground on this continent that has been so often in past times trodden by feet of armed men in conflict of war, as that in the scene before us. We are unable to speak of the overthrow of Iroquois power here at Stadacona, which we know must have taken place about the time that Hochelaga fell. But we have record of the blockade of Quebec by the Iroquois, and the atrocities they committed in the country before us, twenty years after the death of Champlain, and the battle of Sillery Wood, where the British forces, reduced in number after the capture of Quebec, on the following spring were defeated with heavy loss by the French regulars and militia ably led by M. de Levi ; the siege that followed, but failed owing to the arrival of British ships ; and later, the occupation of St. Foye, on the plateau before us, by Arnold and Montgomery, their brief siege of Quebec, and the disastrous failure of their attempt to capture it, already mentioned. But it is chiefly the famous battle of 13th Sept. 1759, to which the Plains of Abraham owe their renown.

What a striking scene the field before us, then an open waste, must have presented that morning. Montcalm's army of five brave French regiments, or battalions of them, with militia in considerable numbers, deploying in oblique line in the fore-ground. Immediately before us are the regiments of "Languedoc," "Guienne" and "Bearne." They are led by the heroic Montcalm, of whom, from his valorous past career, it might be said, as of the Douglas of old, "A doughtier bairn there ne'er was born." How gallant and noble he looks, on his dark horse, in the graceful French uniform of the time. His fine wristband cambric shows copiously under his wide, richly laced sleeve, as he raises his sword aloft, ordering the commencement of battle. His troops, firing by platoons as they go, advance with great dash and resolution towards their antagonists over beyond the towers now there ; but Wolfe's picked battalions waver not ; their fire has been steadily reserved till, at forty paces distance, it is poured in on their advancing assailants, and maintained with deadly rapidity and effect, causing manifest disorder. Brief and very severe is the fighting. Wolfe has fallen ! His successor is wounded, almost mortally ; the command has passed to a third general. Montcalm is wounded, and his second in command has fallen. Then, through the rising smoke of their last volley, is seen the gleaming line of levelled bayonets of Wolfe's Louisbourg Grenadiers advancing in rapid charge ; and on their left the Highlanders, who have thrown away their muskets and taken to their broadswords, are now—

"With tartans waving far and wide,
"And claymores glittering clear."

in swift and deadly pursuit that allows no rally, till the routed remains of Montcalm's army are driven to the gates of the town and to the River St. Charles.

The "slogan" of "claymore" was a very critical war cry in those days to all concerned.

The ranks of the best British regiments in superior numbers had gone down before it, fighting hard, or given way, a few years before; and so well might others who found that unusual style of fighting barbarous and embarrassing. Its effective nature and their ready daring led to their being employed for services especially dangerous. Their loss thereby in this fight, as in others, being proportionally double that of the other British troops.

But apart from their important share in this battle, and the singularly scenic effect of their costume and action, their presence here is noteworthy in an archæological point of view, this being one of the latest of important battles in which was displayed in effective action their ancient national weapon—the identical great broadsword described by Tacitus, as used in the same daring manner by their Caledonian ancestors eighteen hundred years ago, and with which they maintained their national independence against the utmost efforts of the Romans for centuries thereafter.

Montcalm's army actually engaged in this battle was unquestionably much inferior to Wolfe's in effective force of regular troops. Indeed, such was the actual disparity in that respect against him, as to lead the French Viceroy to consider his giving battle an act of chivalrous indiscretion. But we must remember that he repulsed Wolfe at Montmorenci shortly before, and had been victorious over superior numbers in the earlier part of this war.

It was a sternly fought battle, without loss of honour on either side, between small but brave armies, under leaders of immortal renown:—the stake, continental empire, the result, the ultimate establishment of constitutional government and the union of the descendants of the combatants into a common prosperous nationality of great future promise. It was in manifestation of community of feeling that the monument, we just before passed, was erected in commemoration of both the heroic leaders, and surely more appropriate Latin was never written than when Dr. Fisher penned the inscription:—

MORTEM. VIRTUS. COMMVNEM.
FAMAM. HISTORIA.
MONVMENTVM. POSTERITAS.
DEDIT.

Before leaving the battle-field, a personal reminiscence, relating to one of the last of Montcalm's soldiers hitherto unrecorded, may, perhaps, not be out of place.

Over fifty years ago, on a bright frosty evening late in the fall, there came a small party or family group of Abenaquis Indians to my father's house, that stood alone on the skirt of that blue mountain, that dips backward with a faint-jog to the southern horizon. On being asked where they came from they said: " From the west," pointing to the remote high hills behind which the ruddy sun was setting. They said they were cold and hungry. My father brought them in to warm and feed. The patriarch, or chief, was a very aged, superior looking man. As he stood in front of the blazing log fire around which the others were squatted, I saw he was not an Indian, and asked in what parish he was born. I shall never forget his look and attitude as he replied : " Suis pas Canadien ; suis Français," and proceeded, in not very perfect English, to say that he was born at Rouen, on the Seine ; that he was a soldier of the Regiment of Roussillon : that in the war against the English, before the taking of Quebec, he had been much with the Indians engaged in it ; and that after the conclusion of the war, he remained with them. Pointing to a very old and bent little woman sitting at the left side of the fire, he said she was his wife, and was an English girl that he had rescued when the Indians he was with, had massacred a small settlement of "Bostonois," including her parents, who had come from England the year before, when she was twelve years old. On a few words being addressed to her in English, she stared vacantly, and she said she had lost all that long ago and spoke only Indian now. Her features were not Indian.

I have seen, when a boy, men who had fought at Culloden; but they lived in the ordinary walks of life, in civilized society, in the land of their childhood, with old friends and compeers around them; they would die and their ashes would lie with their fathers, or in the land of their birth. But he was far from his kindred; for an ordinary life time, his surroundings had been the lonely forests and savage men. The land of his birth would never more be seen by him; his fair native town by the banks of the Seine, and the associations of his youth would be to him a misty dream; and far away back in the past, would be his recollections of the banner of France and his gallant commander. Such might be the unique and sombre recollections of the last follower of Montcalm, the last soldier of "Louis Quinze" in Canada.

I have touched but lightly on the more modern historical associations of Quebec. To embrace all its grand and profoundly interesting reminiscences we must go back to the days of the men to whom the last "War of the Rose" and the battle of "Bosworth" were as recent events as "Austerlitz" and "Waterloo" are to us; and the "Sac of Rome by the Bourbon" as recent as the Siege of Sebastopol—back to the days of the grandfathers of the men that fought at "Moncontour" and "Ivry"! to the days of romantic discovery, when the most advanced of civilized European nations first came in contact here with "prehistoric man" of this continent.

A. J. R.

Ottawa, 5th Feb., 1876.

MARINE & EMIGRANT HOSPITAL.
Built in 1834.

QUEBEC.

Lines suggested by reading the patriotic historical article recently written by "A. J. R.," based upon the idea of Lord Dufferin, for the rehabilitation of Quebec.

What ? Strip Quebec of her walls of might,
And rob her name of the grandeur bright
That shed a halo of glory o'er
Her battlements in the days of yore—
A lustre far beyond the beams
Which gilded Stadacona's dreams,
When lake and mountain, stream and hill,
Wild cataract and shining rill,
The elk, the bison and the bear,
The moose, the panther in his lair—
The waterfowl that cleaves the sky,
And all the wild wood's minstrelsy,
From sunrise to his setting ray,
Acknowledged the proud Indian's sway ?
What ? Raise the bastion and tear the sod
Where Wolfe's embattled legions trod.
And over Abraham's deathless plain
Unfurled the meteor of the main—
The Red Cross banner of the brave—
And in the hour of triumph gave
A Kingdom's mighty breadth to gem
Old England's glittering diadem !
Forget the bold and sorrowing few

Who' round the striken warrior drew,
To contemplate with streaming eyes
The glory where a hero dies !
The solemn Iroquois whose breast
Is in the hues of battle drest,
Bending in grief his chieftain's crest,
The tartan'd Scot with quivering lips
Gazing on young life's dark eclipse,
The flank man of the grenadiers,
Who listens to the ringing cheers,
While mists of sorrow cloud his sight
To the stern glories of the fight,
Which tells a well fought battle won,
And Wolfe's last day of glory done !
Dismantle the old ramparts grey,
That held Montgomery at bay ;
And foiled the traitor Arnold's power
In Canada's most gloomy hour,
When banded hosts from foreign soil
Sought to o'erturn and despoil,
And wrench with fierce invading hand
The trophy of Wolfe's gallant band
From hearts which nobly, proudly, well
Guarded the trust that o'er them fell.
When brave Montcalm, in battle's van,
Died ! while the Scotish slogan ran
Along each serried kilted clan,
And the fell claymore, dyed all o'er.
Flash'd red with vanquish'd foeman's gore !
Never ! no, never ! while a ray

Of patriot's glory lights our way
Back down the vista that is gone,
Can such a vandal deed be done !
What ? break the link, the brightest, best
That binds us to our mother's breast—
Cut the strong gordian knot in twain
Whose tendons reach across the main,
Destroy with sacrilegious hand
The proudest record of the land,
Consign to dark eternal gloom
The spot where fadeless laurels bloom ?
No ! never, while one throb remains
That keeps a Briton's limbs from chains !
Gibraltar of our northern land
Where British valor made her stand,
And on thy battlements unfurl'd
Her flag defiant to the world !
We love the memories which cling
Round thy old towers—a sacred thing
To every Briton's soul—the strand
Where Wolfe gave up his last command,
And left, with heroism sublime,
His fame—a legacy to Time !

WILLIAM PITTMAN LETT.

Ottawa, 14th Feb. 1876.

THE RIVER SAGUENAY AND ITS SALMON FISHING.

> Methinks the spirits of the brave,
> Who on thy banks have found a grave,
>   Still linger, loath to fly ;
> And on the moanings of the gale
> Strange shapes ride forth, all cold and pale,
>   Unseen by heedless eye.
>
> Oft in mine ears hath darkly rung
> Their solemn requiem, softly sung—
>   Mysterious, deep, and chill,
> And, dying oft, come back again,
> In sweet, unearthly, ghostly strain—
>   The mournful night-winds o'er the hill.   K. K. K.

The interior of the wild country watered by the River Saguenay, was better known, strange to say, two hundred years ago, in the days of the Jesuit missionaries Crespeuil and Albanel, than in the present age. Few white men had wandered over these silen wastes which echoed to the warwhoops of the Monta gnais and Nascapé Indians, sole masters of this boundless territory.

Jacques Cartier had cast anchor, 'tis true, at Tadoussac on 1st September, 1535. The flattering accounts he subsequently published, of the mineral riches of the Saguenay country, were derived from the Indian chief Donacona, who repeated the same assertions when brought in the presence of the French monarch Francis I. In Champlain's time (1610), mention is made of a renowned Montagnais Sagamo, named *Anadabijou,* who had an interview with

Champlain and Lescarbot, at *Pointe-aux-Bouleaux*, about one mile west of Tadoussac.

In the course of my Waltonian rambles in the lower St. Lawrence, I have seen nature in her blandest forms; I have seen her also in all her rugged beauty. No where, ever, have I been more impressed with her grim majesty than in ascending the deep, black waters of the Saguenay. Reader, have you ever felt, on a bright June morning, or on a pensive September afternoon, the awful solitude of the spot? Did you never, in fact, face the " terrors of the Saguenay?" Lest I might underrate them, let me borrow from an able account, penned by a European tourist (Mr. Wood, the special correspondent of the London *Times*), who formed one of the Prince of Wales's party in the English ship-of-war, *Flying Fish:*

" Gloomy black clouds rested on the mountains, and seemed to double their height, pouring over the rugged cliffs in a stream of mist, till, lifting suddenly with the hoarse gusts of wind, they allowed short glimpses into what may almost be called the terrors of the Saguenay scenery. It is on such a day, above all others, that the savage wildness and gloom of this extraordinary river is seen to the greatest advantage. Sunlight and clear skies are out of place over its black waters. Anything which recalls the life and smile of nature is not in unison with the huge naked cliffs, raw, cold, and silent as tombs. An Italian spring could effect no change in its deadly rugged aspect; nor does winter add an iota to its mournful desolation. It is a river which one should see if only to know what dreadful aspects Nature can assume in her wild moods. Once seen, however, few will care to visit it again, for it is with a sense of relief that the tourist emerges from its sullen gloom, and looks back upon it as a kind of vault—nature's sarcophagus, where life sound seems never to have entered. Compared to it, the Dead Sea is blooming, and the wildest ravines look cosy and smiling. It is wild without the least variety, and grand apparently in spite of itself; while so utter is the solitude, so dreary and monotonous the frown of its great black walls of rock, that the tourist is sure to get impatient with its sullen dead reverse, till he feels almost an antipathy to its very name. Some six miles above is the little town, or, as in England we should call it, village of Tadousac. It is more than 300 years since Jacques Cartier, the discoverer of Canada, the bold adventurer, who, through his misinterpretation of the Indian word "welcome," gave the present name to the country, landed here. It was almost his first real resting-place; and the first mention which we have of the Saguenay is one which now well befits its savage aspect, for Cartier sent a boat and crew to explore its rocky chasm, which he never more heard of. From that day to this, the river has had a name which, allowing for the difference of times and creeds, only Styx can equal. At the mouth of the Saguenay the water varies in depth from ten to sixteen fathoms;

but once between the walls of the river, and the depth from end to end is never less than 100 fathoms, generally 150. On either side, at a distance of obout a mile apart, the cliffs rise up thin, white, and straight, varying in perpendicular height from 1,200 to 1,600 feet; and this is the character of the river Saguenay from its mouth to its source. On the right bank, the cliffs are wholy mantled here and there with stunted pines; but on the left, there is scarcely a sign of life or verdure; and the limestone rock stick up white and bleached in the gloomy air, like the bones of an old world.

" At two places, St. Marguerite and betwen Capes Trinity and Eternity, where smaller tributaries pour their contributions into the deep, black stream, a breach occurs in the wall of rocks, as if some giant hand had torn them forcibly back, and left them strewn and baffled of their power in uncouth lumps over the valleys beyond. But these are the only openings, the only means of escape, if they may be so called, from the silent gloom of this dread river. The Saguenay seems to want painting, wants blowing up, or draining — anything, in short, to alter its morose, eternal, quiet awe. Talk of Lethe- of the Styx, they must have been purling brook, compared with this savage river, and a pic-nic on the banks of either would be preferable to one on the Saguenay ! On the occasion of the Prince of Wales' first visit, on the 14th, 1860, the mist and rain hid half its gloom, but more than enough was seen to send the party back to the "Hero" at about five o'clock wet and dull. There was rather a state dinner on board the flagship that evening, and the Prince, having to be up early the next morning, retired at twelve.

"Before six a. m. he was again on board the Governor's steamer, and away up the Saguenay to fish. Before he left, Captain Hope, of the "Flying Fish," had received orders to get up steam and take all the officers of the squadron on an excursion up the river. Of course, every body wished to go, and as the day was bright and glorious, everybody that could come, came. The "Flying Fish" thus had the honour of being the first man-of-war that ever passed up the Saguenay, and if the whole navy of England is sent, I am sure a merrier party will never enter its waters than steamed up on that occasion. Even the Saguenay could not depress their spirits, and if that was not a proof of the zest with which all entered into the day's enjoyment it would be hard to say what was. From St. Marguerite, the smart little sloop steamed on to where the wild scenery of the river culminates at a little inlet on the right bank between Capes Trinity and Eternity. Than these two dreadful headlands nothing can be imagined more grand or more impressive. For one brief moment, the rugged character of the river is partly softened, and, looking back into the deep valley between the capes, the land has an aspect of life and wild luxuriance which, though not rich, at least seems so in comparison with the grievous, awful barrenness. Cape Trinity on the side towards the landward opening is pretty thickly clothed with fir and birch, mingled together in a colour contrast which is beautiful enough, especially when the rocks show out among them, with their little cascades and waterfalls like strips of silver shining in the sun. But Cape Eternity well becomes its name, and is the very reverse of all this. It seems to frown in gloomy indignation on its brother cape for the weakness it betrays in allowing anything like life or verdure to shield its wild, uncouth deformity of strength. Cape Eternity certainly shows no sign of relaxing in this respect from its deep savage grandeur. It is one tremendous cliff of limestone, more than 1500 feet, high, and inclining forward nearly 200 feet, browbeating all beneath it, and seeming as if at any moment it would fall and overwhelm the deep black stream which flows down so cold, so deep and motionless below. High up, on its rough gray brows, a few stunted pines show like bristles their scathed white arms, giving an awful, weird aspect to the mass, blanched here and there by the tempests of ages, stained and discoloured by little waterfalls, in blotchy and decaying spots, but all speaking mutely of a long-gone time when the Saguenay was old, silent and gloomy, before England was known, or the name of Christianity understood. Unlike Niagara, and all other of God's great works in nature, one does not wish for silence or solitude here. Companionship becomes doubly necessary in an awful solitude like this, and though you involuntarily talk in subdued .

tones, still talk you must, if only to relieve your mind of the feeling of loneliness and desolation which seems to weigh on all who venture up this stern, grim, watery chasm.

"The 'Flying Fish' passed under this cape slowly with her yards almost touching the rock, though with more than a thousand feet of water under her. Even the middies and youngsters from the squadron were awed by the scene into a temporary quietness. The solemn and almot forbidden silence at last became too much. The party said they had not come out to be overawed, chilled, and subdued by rocks, however tremendous, so it was carried *nem. con.* that, dead and stony as they were, they must at least have echoes, and the time was come to wake them. In a minute after, and Captain Hope having good-naturedly given his consent, one of the largest 68-pounders was cast loose and trained aft to face the cliff. From under its overhanging mass the 'Flying Fish' was moved with care, lest any loose crag shouldbe sufficiently disturbed by the concussion to come down bodily upon her decks. A safe distance thus gained, the gun was fired. None who were in the 'Flying Fish' that day will ever forget its sound. For the space of a half a minute or so after the discharge, there was a dead silence, and then, as if the report and concussion were hurled back upon the decks, the echoes came down crash on crash. It seemed as if the rocks and crags had all sprung into life under the tremendous din, and as if each was firing 68-pounders full upon us, in sharp, crushing volleys, till at last they grew hoarser in their anger, and retreated, bellowing slowly, carrying the tale of invaded solitude from hill to hill, till all the distant mountains seemed to roar and groan at the intrusion. It was the first time these hideous cliffs had ever been made to speak, and when they did break silence they did it to some purpose.

A few miles further on, the "Flying Fish" passed under Statue Point, where, at about 1000 feet above the water a huge rough Gothic arch gives entrance to a cave in which, as yet, the foot of man has never trodden. Before the entrance to this black aperture a gigantic rock, like the statue of some dead Titan, once stood. A few years ago, during the winter, it gave way, and the monstrous figure came crashing down through the ice of the Saguenay, and left bare to view the entrance to the cavern it had guarded perhaps for ages. Beyond this, again, was the Tableau Rock, a sheet of dark-coloured limestone, some 600 feet high by 300 wide, as straight and almost as smooth as a mirror."

THE BASILICA MINOR.

The walls of this Church, are decorated with finepaintings, of which follows a list enumerated in order, commencing the survey to the right from the entrance, following the passage along the pillars which divide the nave from the wings.

I. The Holy Family, by Blanchard (1600-1630 painter to the king of France.)
II. The Saviour insulted by the soldiers,—St. Matthews, XXVII, 27, 31,—by Fleuret. (French school.)
III. Birth of Christ, a splendid copy of the celebrated by Annibal Carrache. (Italian school).
IV. The Flight of Joseph into Egypt, a copy of the original by Vanloo Flemish school) in the Seminary Chapel, by Theophile Hamel.
V. Our Saviour attended to by the Angels after the temptation in the desert, by Restout, 1692-1718, french school).
VI. The Immaculate Conception, Lebrun's (french school) style.
VII. St. Paul's extacy, by Carlo Maretti (1625-1713) Italian school).
VIII. Altar: Miracles of St. Ann, by A. Plamondon, canadian artist and a pupil of Paul Guérin.
IX. Our Saviour on the Cross, by Van Dyck (1599-1641, flemish school). This painting is one of the most remarkable in America and perhaps the best in Canada.
X. The Pentecost by Vignon (french school.)
XI. The Annunciation, by Restout, french school.)
XII. Lying into the Sepulchre, copied by A. Plamondon, from the original by Hutin, in the Seminary chapel.
XIII. The Baptism of Christ, by Claude Guy Hallé (1652-1736, french school.) The sacristy contains the wards of the church, the rich ornaments given to Bishop Laval by Louis XV.

The entrance to the chapel of the Seminary, is through that of the Seminary, where a door-keeper, receives the

visitors and accompanies them to the chapel containing the paintaings indicated below and enumerated in order, pursuing the survey on the right hand, from the entrance :
I. The Saviour and the woman of Samaria at Jacob's Well, near Sychar, St. John, IV, by Lagrenée.
II. The virgin ministered unto by the angels, who are represented as preparing the linen clothes for the child Jesus, by Dieu.
III. In the lateral chapel, on the right, a large figure of the Saviour on the cross, at the precise moment described by the Evangelist St. John, XIX, 30,—by Moucy.
IV. At the entrance, the Egyptian Hermits, in the solitude of Thebais,—by Guillot.
V. In the chancel, the terror of St. Jerome, at the recollection of a vision of the day of judgment,—by D'Hullin. (copy).
VI. The Ascension of our Lord Jesus-Christ,—by P. Champagne.
VII. The Saviour's sepulchre and interment,—by Hutin.
VIII. Above the Altar, the flight of Joseph to Egypt. St. Matthew, by Vanloo. Immediately above, is a small oval picture delineating two Angels, by Lebrun.
IX. The trance of St. Anthony, on beholding the child Jesus, by Parrocel d'Avignon.
X. The day of Pentecost. Acts II, by Champagne.
XI. St. Peters, delivrance from prison. Acts XII,—by De la Fosse.
XII. At the entrance of the lateral chapel on the left, another view of the Hermits of Thebais, by—Guillot.
XIII. In the rear, the baptism of Christ. St. Mathew, III, —by Claude Guy Hallé.
XIV. St. Jerome writing, by J. B. Champagne.
XV. The wise man of the East adoring the Saviour. St. Matthew II,—by Bounier.

The shrine on the right of the chief altar contains the Relics of St. Clement ; that, on the left, the Relics of St. Modestus. This chapel was erected about a century ago.

MEMORABILIA.

Jacques-Cartier landed on the banks of the Saint Charles.................................... Sept 14, 1535
Quebec founded by Samuel de Champlain...July 3, 1608
Fort St. Louis built at Quebec..................... 1620
Quebec surrendered to Admiral Kirk.............. 1629
Quebec returned to the French..................... 1632
Death of Champlain, the first Governor....Dec. 25, 1635
Settlement formed at Sillery....................... 1637
A Royal Government formed at Quebec............ 1663
Quebec unsuccessfully besieged by Admiral Phipps.. 1690
Count de Frontenac died...................Nov. 28, 1698
Battle of the Plains of Abraham..........Sept. 13, 1759
Capitulation of Quebec...................Sept. 18, 1759
Battle of St. Foye—a French victory......April 28, 1760
Canada ceded by treaty to England................ 1763
Blockade of Quebec by Generals Montgomery and Arnold...............................Nov. 10, 1775
Death of Montgomery....................31st Dec. 1775
Retreat of Americans from Quebec..........May 6, 1776
Division of Canada into Upper and Lower Canada.. 1791
Insurrection in Canada............................ 1837
Second Insurrection............................... 1838
Union of the two Provinces in one................. 1840
Dominion of Canada formed............... July 1, 1867
Departure of English troops....................... 1870
Second Centenary of Foundation of Bishopric of Quebec by Monseigneur Laval....Oct 1 1674, 1874
Centenary of Repulse of Arnold and Montgomery before Quebec on 31st Dec. 1775—31st Dec. 1875
Dufferin Plans of City embellishment, Christmas day. 1875

TARIFF OF CARTERS OF LIGHT VEHICLES.

CARRIAGES FOR HIRE.	TARIFF FOR HACKNEY CARRIAGES.					
	Two horses Vehicles.		One horse vehicles.			
			Waggon.		Calesh.	
	One or two persons.	Three or four persons.	One or two persons.	Three or four persons.	One person.	Two persons.
From any place to any other place within the city limits..........	$1 00	$1 50	$0 50	$0 75	$0 20	$0 40
If to go and return, add 50 per cent to the above rates. When the drive exceeds the hour, hour rates to be charged **BY THE HOUR.**						
For the first hour................	1 00	1 00	0 75	1 00	0 50	0 60
Each additional hour............	0 75	1 00	0 50	0 75	0 40	0 50

Provided however the rate per day of 24 hours shall not in any case exceed five dollars for a calesh, seven dollars fifty cents for a waggon, or ten dollars for a carriage drawn by two horses.

Fractions of hours to be charged at pro rata hour rates, but not less than one-quarter of an hour shall be charged when the time exceeds the hour.

Fifty per cent to be added to the tariff rates from midnight to 4 A. M.

The tarif by the hour shall apply to all drives extending beyond the City limits when the engagement is commenced and concluded within the city.

BAGGAGE.

For each trunk or box carried in any vehicle, 5 cents; but no charge shall be made for travelling bags or valises which passengers can carry by the hand.

BELLEVUE CONVENT,

St. Foye's road, Quebec.

THE SAGUENAY

AND

LOWER ST. LAWRENCE.

In order to help tourists in forming an idea of what a trip down the St. Lawrence and Saguenay rivers is worth, and how it is made, we quote from the *Boston Journal* the narrative written by one of the members of the Massachusett Press Association after an excursion to those places :—

OFF FOR THE SAGUENAY.

The crowning feature of the excursion was a trip up the romantic Saguenay river. The party left Quebec Tuesday morning in the fine steamer *Saguenay*, Captain Michel Lecours, of the St. Lawrence Steam Navigation Company's line, which maintains almost daily communication with Ha! Ha! Bay and Chicoutimi during the season of summer travel. It chanced to be the opening trip of the *Saguenay* for the present year, and everything about the vessel was in the best of order. The assignment of quarters had already

been made by President Merrill of the excursion
party and the purser of the steamer, Mr. Joseph
St. Onge, and everybody was soon made at home.
An excellent breakfast was one of the early incidents of the trip, and in this connection I would
remark that an elegant and substantial bill of fare,
in which delicious and fresh salmon invariably
figures, is served on the *Saguenay*, and I presume
on the other boats of the line. The other steamers
which ply between Quebec and the Saguenay are
the *Union*, Captain Hamond, and the *St. Lawrence*, Captain Chabot.

THE SCENERY ON THE ST. LAWRENCE.

The view of Quebec from below the city is ex-
ceedingly fine. The Upper Town is built upon
a northeasterly slope, and not only the citadel
which crowns the hill, but the tin-roofed church
spires and buildings of the whole upper section,
and also the Lower Town from in front of the
citadel around to St. Roch's and St. John's
suburbs, are at once seen. The only complete
view of Quebec, in fact, is had from the river below the city, or from the hights on the opposite
side of the River St. Charles. Soon after leaving
the city, as the steamer approaches the southwesterly point of the Isle of Orleans (which old
Jacques Cartier in 1535 christened the Isle of
Bacchus), the white veil of the Montmorency Fall
is in plain view, several miles distant. The Isle
of Orleans, twenty one miles in length, and in

some places five miles wide, is covered by fine farms, and much of the garden produce which finds its way to the Quebec market is here raised. A ferry boat plies between the city and the island, and furnishes the means of communication with the outer world for five or six populous parishes. Below the Isle of Orleans the St. Lawrence broadens into the semblance of a great lake, and the scenery along its banks changes greatly. The main channel of the river is in the south side of Orleans, but the steamer's course after passing the island is along the northerly shore. The other boats of the line pass more to the south, as Murray Bay is their first stopping place. There are populous villages on the north shore as far as St. Joachim, near the mouth of Ste. Anne's River, which empties into the St. Lawrence twenty-four miles below Quebec, but the mountainous country below is sparsely settled. The south shore from Quebec to River du Loup, and indeed for an hundred miles below that place to Metis, is well populated, and there are several large parishes upon the river bank, l'Islet, Kamouraska, River du Loup and Rimouski being of the number. On the north shore the outlayers of the Laurentian mountains approach the river, and there are some precipitous hills which rise from the water's edge, and adown which trickle romantic cascades. Ste. Anne, the highest of the Laurentian range seen from the river, is 2687 feet high. It is situated nearly twenty miles from the river, nearly opposite the lower point of the Isle of Orleans. Cape Tourmente, which rises from the water's edge, twenty-eight miles from Quebec, is a prominent object in the down-river view from Quebec. Its hight is 1919 feet. Cape Gribaune, eight or ten miles below Cape Tourmente, is still higher—2171 feet. Cape Maillard is a lesser peak, which rises near the mouth of the River Bouchard and the little settlement of St. François-Xavier.

The first stopping place of our steamer is at St. Paul's Bay, a parish of about 1500 inhabitants, at the mouth of the river Gouffre, and opposite the upper part of the Isle aux Coudres, fifty-five miles below Quebec. There is no pier at this place and the steamer is compelled to exchange the mails and passengers by swinging up alongside a small schooner which is anchored some distance from the shore. Back of St. Paul's in the parish of St. Urbain are some iron mines and and a rolling mill, not now in operation, and there are said to be some valuable iron diposits on the Isle aux Coudres, which is about six miles long and has a population of about two hundred souls. This island was granted to the ecclesiastics of the Seminary of Quebec as long ago as 1687, and is still held by them.

The next landing place is Les Eboulements, eleven miles below St. Paul's Bay, and sixty-six miles from Quebec. This place has a farming population of 300 or 400, and is situated near the foot of Mount Eboulements, which has an elevation of 2547 feet. As we approach Les Eboulements the mountain's crest is draped with clouds and fleecy formations drift along its sides. There is a good pier at this place and another at Murray Bay, sixteen miles below, which is the next landing place.

Murray Bay, or Malbaie, eighty-two miles below Quebec, not only has a population of some 2000 of its own, but in summer it has a large number of fashionable visitors from Quebec and Montreal. The summer residences are chiefly at Point a Pique and Cape a L'Aigle, on either side of the old settlement, and at the former, near where the steamer's landing place is situated, there are three hotels—the Lorn House, Du Berger's Hotel and the Warren House. Although Murray Bay is some six hundred miles from the Atlantic Ocean, " sea bathing " is one of its chief attractions.

From Murray Bay the steamer takes a diagonal course across to the south shore, where Rivière du Loup is situated thirty miles below, and one hundred and twelve miles from Quebec. The village, which is situated two or three miles back of the long pier, presents a very pleasant appearrance on the approach by the river, and its charms are greatly enhanced on a closer inspection. There are some romantic falls back of the village. A branch of the Grand Trunk Railway runs to Riviere du Loup from Point Levis, opposite Quebec, and the new Intercolonial Railway, which is to connect the Lower Provinces with Quebec, has been opened sixty-miles below to Rimouski. This latter is one of the most thoroughly built roads in

America. Cacouna, the most famous watering place on the St. Lawrence, is situated six or eight miles below the landing place at Rivière de Loup. There is a large hotel at this place, St. Lawrence Hall, which was formerly kept by Mr. Hogan, of the St. Lawrence Hall, Montreal, but is now in other hands.

A GORGEOUS SUNSET.

From Rivière du Loup the steamer takes a diagonal course across the St. Lawrence to Tadousac, which is situated at the mouth of the Saguenay. The distance between the two points is twenty-two miles, the actual width of the river being about fifteen miles. A most glorious sunset was enjoyed on the way over. Leaden clouds hung like a canopy over the St. Lawrence, but the northwesterly shore marked their limit and beyond was the clear sun-lit sky. Deep, black clouds which hung about the mountains off toward Murray Bay seemed to indicate that the showers which had been encountered in the early afternoon near Mount Eboulements were still playing about the lofty elevations in that direction. A long range of clouds, beautiful in their rounded outlines and snowy whiteness, hung along the course of the Saguenay and beyond, seemingly marking the course of mighty river. Their tobs were illumined by the declining sun and were soon flushed with a purple hue as the orb of day sank behind the horizon, while little fleecy masses which were more directly in his path were enriched by still brighter coloring. Added to the enchanting celestial scenery were the distant blue mountain ridges on the north shore, the broad, majestic river, and the numerous islands, which stud its expanse above and below Riviere du Loup, from Hare Island, the Pilgrim Isles and the " Brandy Pots " down to the lovely groups off Isle Verte and Trois Pistoles—the whole forming a picture of unsurpassed beauty. In these northern latitudes the days are longer than with us, and after 9 o'clock, long after we had entered the black waters of the Saguenay, it was possible to read ordinary print in the twilight.

Although the historian Pinkerton tells us that an expedition was fitted out under De Roberval for the exploration of the Saguenay river as early as 1543, very little has been known of it, or of the interesting country through which it courses, until quite recently. Bouchette made some valuable explorations of the river and its sources in the early part of the present century, and these form the basis of all modern maps and topographical descriptions. Of the results of De Roberval's expedition, which numbered eight barges and seventy men, nothing is known beyond the fact that one of the vessels and eight men were lost. In 1599, Sieur de Chauvin made a futile attempt to settle on the Saguenay, and Champlain records that he died at Tadousac, or Tadoussac, as all the old anthorities spell the name. The exclusive right to trade in the Saguenay country was ceded to Sieur Demonts in 1658, and in 1733 the limit of these concessions was defined to extend from the lower end of the Eboulements to Cape Cormorant, a distance of eighty leagues along the St. Lawrence front.

Before entering upon a recital of our own pleasant experiences upon this mighty river of the north, it would be well to glance at the map and trace the course of this, the greatest of the tributaries of the St. Lawrence. The Saguenay proper flows from Lake St. John, a large body of water, of nearly circular shape, some forty odd miles across, which is situated just below the 49th degree of north latitude and on the 72d degree of longitude, west. The northerly feeders of the lake rise in the range of mountains which divides Canada from British North America. The waters of Lake Mistassini, which lies a short distance north of these mountains, flow into Hudson's Bay. The farthermost sources of the Saguenay are some two hundred miles west of Lake St. John. There are eleven rivers flowing into Lake St. John, and nineteen other tributaries add their waters to the Saguenay between the lake and the St. Lawrence. Of the rivers flowing into the lake, the chief are the Assuapmoussoin, Mistassini (which has no connection with the lake of the same name), Peribonca (or Curious river), Ouiatshoanish, and the Metabetshouan (near the mouth of which are the chief settlements, originally foundered by the Jesuits). Of the thirty rivers which are tributary to the Saguenay, twelve are navigable by canoes,

The Saguenay is navigable for ships of the largest class to within nine miles of Chicoutimi, which is ninety-four miles from the mouth, and large steamers have no difficulty in reaching Chicoutimi, advantage being taken of the tides and of the channel, which is marked by buoys. The distance from Chicoutimi to Lake St. John is about sixty miles, and navigation ceases at the Rapids of Terres Rompues, about nine miles above Chicoutimi, where the tides also end. At Ha! Ha! Bay the spring tides rise eighteen feet and at the mouth of the Saguenay their hight is twenty-one feet. The general course of the river is E. S. E., but it is often diverted from a direct course by the jutting points of rock. The Saguenay flows between two mountain ranges, which rise from the water's edge, and is immensely deep. At the mouth, where the banks are more contracted than they are above, it has been impossible to find bottom with 500 fathoms of line, and there are other places where no soundings are had. Indeed, the only anchorage grounds between Tadousac and Ha! Ha! Bay are at the mouth of the River Ste. Marguerite, fifteen miles from the mouth, and in St. John's Bay, seventeen miles above the last-named point. The Ste. Marguerite, which is one of the largest of the rivers flowing into the Saguenay below Lake St. John, is noted for its salmon fisheries, which are leased of the Government by Mr. Willis Russell of the St. Louis Hotel, Quebec, and Mr. Powell of Philadelphia.

Posts for trading with the Indians were early

established at Tadousac, Chicoutimi, Lake St. John, the Isles de Jeremie, near Betsiamits, and at various other points. They were called King's Posts. Together with the privileges pertaining thereto, these posts were leased to a corporation of Scotch merchants known as the Northwest Company, who at length united their fortunes to those of the Hudson Bay Company. Within a few years past still further changes have taken place, the Hudson Bay Company having ceased to exist in its old form. All the old posts about the St. Lawrence and the Saguenay have been discontinued except that near Betsiamits, which is on the north side of the St. Lawrence, about fifty miles below Tadousac. Furs in considerable quantities are carried to Tadousac every spring and shipped to Quebec by steamer.

The Indians who formerly occupied the country about the Saguenay were the Montagnais, the descendants of the powerful Algonquins. Disease and the excessive use of fire-water have depleted the ranks of the red men, and their number is now small. In 1824 there were altogether not over 700 of them, a decrease of 300 in twenty years.

The Saguenay is generally frozen over from the St. Louis Isles to the head of navigation about six months in the year. The river was clear of ice this year May 27. There was considerable snow on the mountains as late as June 8, and at the present time a huge patch of snow and ice is to be seen on a mountain side a few miles above Tadoussac.

A NIGHT ASCENT OF THE SAGUENAY.

The Quebec steamers are run on,—at least the *Saguenay*, which takes a somewhat different course than the others—so that the tourist passes the first night in ascending the Saguenay. The boat reaches Ha ! Ha ! Bay at one or two o'clock in the morning and lies in there until seven or eight, when it proceeds up to Chicoutimi, returning to Tadoussac and Riviere du Loup by day, and from thence passing up the St. Lawrence to Quebec during the second night. This programme was carried on this occasion, with the exception that the chief stop was made at Tadoussac on the return instead of going up.

As we rounded out from the harbor at Tadousac soon after sunset and the steamer pointed her prow on the river which gave her a name a severe northwest wind was encountered. It is a somewhat remarkable fact that the only appreciable winds encountered on the Saguenay are from the northwest or the northeast. The wind on this occasion was particularly strong and it drove all save a few adventurous spirits from the deck. One of the doors of the pilot house, carelessly left swinging, was twisted from its hinges in a twinkling by a sudden gust and hurled into the water with several tools from which some of the passengers had just retréated. A short distance from the mouth of the river towering cliffs rise upon either side and directly in front. Tete de Boule is a prominent mountain with a rounded top, which appears to rise from the middle of the river several miles above Tadousac, but the stream it is soon found takes its course to the northward. All the hights about Tadousac bear the marks of devastating fires, and farther up the Saguenay are seen the effects of a terrible forest fire which occurred some sixty years ago, and which destroyed the timber for a broad extent, and the earthly deposits as well, leaving scarcely anything to which subsequent vegetation might cling. The birch hemlock are about the only woods found in close proximity to the river, although many other varieties formerly flourished here in great profusion. Further back on the tributary water courses the forest growth is more profuse, and the lumbering operations, which at present form the only business along the Saguenay, find their sources of supply in those regions. Of these more anon. The mountain near the mouth of the river are of liberal dimensions, but upon the further ascent elevations assume still greater proportions and bolder outlines, until the huge and imposing cliffs of Point Eternity and Cap Trinity, which rise perpendicularly from the water, burst upon the view in all their giant-like and grim grandeur. These points were passed between eleven and twelve o'clock at night on the upward trip, and as a matter of course could not be appreciated by the passengers, some of whom had already retired, while a few timid ones were determined to be "up and dressed" until the boat touched the wharf at Ha! Ha! Bay, which it did about two o'clock. While passing Point Eternity, the little steamer " Samson " was encountered, towing a ship up the river—one of the crafts employed to carry lumber by Mr. Price, to whom the little steamer belongs. The sparks from the " Samson's smoke-stack made a fiery train against the dark back-ground of the huge cliff, adding a weird aspect to the grand spectacle presented by the mountain and its grand surroundings.

HA! HA! BAY.

There is a tradition that Ha! Ha! Bay, or the Baie des Has, derived its title from the exclamations of some of the early explorers who entered it by mistake, supposing it to be the true course of the river instead of an inlet, but it is quite as likely to have come from the Indians who formerly inhabited the country and fished and hunted about its waters. The place is also known as Grand Bay. The aspect of the shores is materially changed at this point, rolling hills with cultivated fields taking the place of the steep and inaccessible mountains which line the river below. There are two parishes on the shores of Ha! Ha! Bay, St. Alphonse, where the steamer lands, containing a population of about 1700, and S. Alexis three miles below, with a population of about 1400. The inhabitants are almost all Canadian French, and consequently Catholics. There is a large church in each place. Usually, when the steamer reaches Ha! Ha! Bay about half the population turns out with *calèches* to treat the passengers to a ride to St. Alexis, or over the hills back of St. Alphonse, while here and there an humble descendant of the Algonquins, who knows French but not her mother Indian tongue, offers beadwork or basket work for sale. In the present instance not a solitary *calèche* or a solitary squaw invaded the wharf. Either our early and unannounced arrival (this was the " Saguenay's " first trip, it will be remembered,) or the fact that everybody was preparing to celebrate St. John's Day, deprived us of a sight of the inhabitants. There is a large saw-mill at St. Alexis, but of other manufactures Ha ! Ha ! Bay can boast of none. The people generally subsist on their own resources. In the early fall large quantities of blueberries and some other fruits, with farm products, are sent to the Quebec market, the annual shipments, perhaps, reaching $15,000. This blueberries, which grow on the neighboring mountain sides in great profusion, are placed in boxes closely ressembling coffins in shape, each box containing a bushel or more. The berries are commonly sold at twenty-five cents a box, and sometimes as low as eight cents a box. There is overland communication with Ha ! Ha ! Bay, Chicoutimi and the Lake St. John settlements in the winter, a road leading down from Quebec through the Laurentian Mountain to Bay St. Paul, Eboulements and Murray Bay, and thence across the country, but in summer a better and more rapid means of transit is furnished by the steamers, and the road is then but little used.

THE LUMBERING ON THE SAGUENAY.

Of late years there has been a large increase in the lumbering operation on the Saguenay under the direction of the Messrs. Price, who own or control thousands upon thousands of acres of the Saguenay lands. Hon. David Price, who is generally known as the " King of the Saguenay," reside at Quebec, William Price at Chicoutimi, John Price at Quebec, and other brothers live abroad and manage the European branches of the business. The Price have mills at Ha ! Ha ! Bay, Chicoutimi, St. John Bay, Tadousac, Rimouski, Little Bergeronne, Escoumins, and at several other points. Little Bergeronne and Escoumins are on the northerly shore of the St. Lawrence, below Tadousac. They also have offices in Quebec and in England. Their business amounts to half a million a year, and last year they loaded thirty-six vessels with lumber for England. This year they will sent out forty ship loads. But for the enterprise of the Messrs. Price the Saguenay would see but little business life.

CHICOUTIMI.

Chicoutimi, or Shekutimish, as the Indians called it, is a place of between 2000 and 3000 inhabitants, at the head of navigation on the

Saguenay. A church was built here by the Jesuit Labrosse as early as 1727, and the Indians were converted to Catholicism in large numbers. The Chicoutimi river, which flows from Lake Kenwangomi, empties into the Saguenay at this point over a beautiful fall of forty or fifty feet, which is in plain view from the steamer wharf. At the parish church which has taken the place of the ancient edifice, high mass was being said in honor of St. John Day, and in several localities about the village flags were flying in honor of the day. The steamer " Saguenay," too was decorated with the English, American and Dominion flags, the Stars and Stripes being shown to Chicoutimi probably for the first time.

DOWN THE SAGUENAY BY DAYLIGHT.

Our stay a Chicoutimi was limitted to an hour by the state of the tide, and at the end of that space, Capt. Lecours turned the steamer's head down the river. The downward trip was pleasanter than that of the evening previous, when we ascended the river in the eyes of a terrific wind. Every inch of the river presents some beautiful scene, but the grandest scenery—Tableau Rocks; Statue Point, Cap Trinity and Point Eternity—was not reached until the early afternoon. Dinner had no attractions compared with the views to be obtained from the steamer's deck, and every eye was strained to catch the first glimpse of those stupendous cliffs, Trinity and Eternity. These are situated on the southwesterly shore of the river, forty-one miles from its mouth and twenty-five miles below Ha! Ha! Bay. Cape Trinity is the upper point, although some of the maps make the strange mistake of putting it down as the lower one. It is a mountain of solid rock, rising in three successive precipices both upon the river and the island sides, each of the precipices being about five hundred feet high. The topmost pinnacle rises to from 1500 to 1700 feet. Upon two of the acclivities of Trinity are profiles, one of which, on the second acclivity, is very clearly defined. These are better seen on approaching the cape from above than from below. Eternity rears its head to the hight of eighteen hundred feet, its sides being partly covered with trees, although on many parts there seems nothing but rocky precipices. It is surprising to see trees growing where there seems scarcely earth enough or even sufficient flat surface to which the roots can cling. Down the sides of Eternity a mountain torrent pours, the white dashing waters having the appearance of perfect stilness in the distance. The recent rains have filled the mountain lakes and streams, and the scores of rivulets and cascades which are seen on the descent of the Saguenay are found to wear their most romantic aspect. The cascade on the side of Eternity is fed by a lake some twenty acres in extent. Between Eternity and Trinity is a broad, deep inlet, called Eternity Bay. It has a depth of hundreds of fathoms a large vessel may approach within a few feet of the huge rock of Cape Trinity, which on this side rises in a sheer precipice, almost overhanging, fully fifteen hundred feet. The "Saguenay" steamed up alongside the cliff and then it was that its awful majesty was realized. How little did man seem in comparison with these eternal edifices, the handiwork of nature's God. " Praise God, from whom all blessing flow" burst almost spontaneously from the lips of the wonder-stricken throng on the steamer's deck, and that glorious song of homage to the Creator seemed never to have had more significance than in presence of some of his greatest works. As we sailed under the broad shadow of Point Eternity the beautiful hymn " Rock of Ages," was sung with equal emphasis and equal significance. The solemnity of the scene was felt by all, and there was a meaning to the sacred words which touched every heart.

Before leaving the bay the wonderful effect of the echo was tried. The wind was so strong, however, that the best results were not obtained. The discharge of a cannon elicited several loud responses from the opposite crags, and the steamer's whistle was also answered with a whole series of shrieks.

The Tableau is a column of dark-colored rock nine hundred feet high, the front surface of which is six hundred feet high and three hundred feet wide. It is situated eight or ten miles above Cape Trinity, on the same side of the river. Nearer still to the capes is Statue Point, a huge precipitous cliff, with an inaccessible cavern far up its craggy side, which might serve as a niche for a statue.

Capt. Lecours took the "Saguenay" farther into Eternity Bay than any steamer ever went before, and subsequently to descending the river among the St. Louis Isles, varied his course by going inside both Roy and Barthelmi Island, where the passage seems scarcely wide enough for a vessel to pass, although the depth of water is sufficient to sink Bunker Hill Monument out of sight. Not far below the River Ste. Marguerite, which flows into the Saguenay from the north, a short distance from the St. Louis Isles, the pilot pointed out the rock where the steamer "Magnet" ran ashore in August, 1869, an incident which one of the passengers bore in vivid remembrance, and which was related in the colums of *The Journal* at that time.

TADOUSAC.

The wharf at Tadousac was reached not far from five o'clock, and an hour was afforded for the passengers to visit the old Jesuit church, the hotel and other points of interest. The hotel, which is a famous place of summer ressort, is kept this year by Mr. G. Lulham of Montreal. It is very pleasantly situated on a bluff overlooking a romantic inlet and beach. Now that Lord Dufferin, the Governor General of Canada, has established his summer residence here and built an expensive habitation, Tadousac will doubtless be more frequented than ever. The steamer line furnishes easy means of communication. Among the private summer residences here are several pretty cottages belonging to Mr. Price, and others owned by Mr. Willis Russell of the St. Louis Hotel, Quebec, Mr. Powell of Philadelphia, and Colonel Rhodes, President of the North Shore Railway. The old church is situated a short distance east of the hotel. It was here the first church in Canada was erected. The ancient edifice was burned, and the present structure, scarcely larger than the original, occupies the same site. The bell is said to be the same which hung above the old church, and two pictures are shown which are said to have been brought from France by the early Jesuits. The present church date back to 1746.

THE RETURN TO QUEBEC.

The return from Tadousac to Quebec was over the same route previously described, and a great part of the passage was accomplished in the night without any incident worthy of special mention. Quebec was reached at an early hour, in ample time for a connection with the Grand Trunk Railway, for which Captain Lecours kindly brought his boat to a landing on the Pointe Levis side instead of at her usual dock on the Quebec side. In closing the account of the Saguenay excursion, the writer cannot but convey the general expression of the journalistic voyagers in thanking Captain Lecours and Purser St. Onge for their personal kindness and courtesy in adding to the enjoyment of one of the most delightful pleasure trips it is possible to take on the American continent.

RAILWAY

AND

NAVIGATION LINES FROM QUEBEC.

Grand Trunk Railway.—This is the only railway line which connects Quebec with the other cities of Canada and the United States. The terminus is on the south shore of the St. Lawrence; but the ferry boat of the Company plies between the terminus at Levis and the ticket and freight office of the Company, on the wharves, in front of Champlain Market, Cul de Sac street.

The eastern branch of the Grand Trunk terminates at Rivière du Loup, 120 miles from Quebec, where it connects with the Intercolonial Railway, which shall extend to Halifax, N. S., but is now opened only as far as Rimouski, 186 miles from Quebec.

To the west the Grand Trunk extends to Sarnia, Province of Ontario, branching at Richmond to Portland, at Sherbrooke, by the Connecticut and Passumpsic Railway to Boston, New York, and all the cities of the Atlantic States; at Montreal to St. John and Rouses-Point and thence, by the Vermont Central and the South Eastern Railway to lake Magog and all the cities of the United States; at Prescott to Ottawa by the St. Lawrence and Ottawa Railway, and to the States by the railways from Ogdensburg; at Belleville to Ottawa and Pembroke, by the Canada Central; and at Toronto to all the cities in the West and to lake Huron by the Northern Railway.—Mr. Shipman is the ticket agent for the Grand Trunk and several other lines: Office: No. 7, Buade street, near the Post Office.

The Richelieu Company's Line.— This is the finest line of steamboats on the St. Lawrence, affording daily communication between Montreal and Quebec, by the fine iron steamers *Quebec* and *Montreal*, commanded the first by Capt. Labelle and the second by Capt. Nelson. It is impossible to find more comfort, politeness and kindness than what is met with on board the steamers of the old, wealthy and popular Richelieu line. One of the boats leave Montreal at 7 p. m. and the other Quebec at 4 p. m. every day, except sundays.

Union Navigation Line.—This line is newly opened, in opposition to the Richelieu Company. Their boats are good, but far from those of the Richelieu, as to speed and comfort : the fare is higher.

St. Lawrence & Saguenay Line. —It connects Quebec with all the ports of the Lower St. Lawrence as far as Rimouski. It is composed of the three fine sea-sounding iron deck steamers *St. Lawrence*, Capt. Lecours, *Saguenay* and *Union*. The comfort enjoyed on board cannot be surpassed, and it is an acknowledged fact that the table on board these steamers is equal to that in the *St. Louis Hotel* and *St. Lawrence Hall*. The steamers of this line always wait the arrival of the Richelieu Company's boats from Montreal and leave at 8 a. m., for the lower ports, generally reaching Rivière du Loup between 4 and 5 p. m., and thence cross over to Tadoussac to ascend the Saguenay during the night and descend it in day time.

The Quebec & Gulf Ports Co's Line—Connects Quebec with the southern ports of the Gulf St. Lawrence and even with St. John N. B. and Halifax N. S.

This Company's boats sail every Tuesday from Quebec, and every alternate Friday from Montreal.

Miles from Quebec.			1st class.	2nd class.
175	to	Father's Point	$ 4.00	$ 2.00
200	"	Métis	5.50	2.50
443	"	Gaspé	10.00	4.00
472	"	Percé	11.00	4.25
543	"	Paspébiac	13.00	5.00
598	"	Dalhousie	14.00	5.50
791	"	Chatham	14.00	6.00
796	"	New Castle	14.00	6.00
991	"	Shediac	15.00	7.00
1021	"	Pictou	16.00	7.50

By this line, american tourists can return *via* Portland and Boston, going down the St. Lawrence and enjoying the fine scenery of the Gulf islands, as far as Monkton, and thence by rail to St. John, to reach the steamers plying between this city and Portland or Boston—or as far as Pictou and thence by rail to Halifax to reach the boats plying between that city and the places mentioned above. This is one of the finest and healthiest trips a tourist can make, and a very cheap one too. The comfort on the steamers of this Company is above what can be wished for.

The tickets for all these lines can be procured at the respective offices of the various Companies, and at Messrs Levi and Stevenson, St. Louis street, opposite St. Louis Hotel and Mr Shipman, Buade street, near the Post Office, General ticket agents.

The trade of St. Roch.

To complete all the informations the tourist must have to visit Quebec with pleasure and advantage, we shall say that tourists wanting to buy anything in furs, jewellery or shoes should visit the establishments of St. Roch, where they will buy everything cheaper, especially those of Mr. Laliberté and of M. Gingras for furs, and of Mr. Jacot, Mr. Brunet and Messrs. Duquet & Dallaire for jewellery.

Bellevue Convent

Under the direction of the Ladies of the Congregation de Notre-Dame.

ST. FOYE ROAD, QUEBEC.

Delightfully situated on the St. Foye road, about two miles from Quebec, on an eminence facing the picturesque valley of the river St. Charles. It is a magnificent fire brick, five storied building, with every modern improvement.

Its excellence as a teaching institution will be readily understood by stating that Bellevue has been placed on an equal footing with Villa-Maria (Moucklands). American parents wishing their daughters to learn the French language in all its purity, could not find a more suitable academy, as Bellevue enjoys the most enviable reputation for teaching the correct prononciation of that elegant language.

The course of study pursued here embraces the French and English languages, with all useful and ornamental branches taught to young ladies of the highest circles. Interference with the religious convictions of protestant pupils is strictly avoided.

The staff of teachers is selected among the 600 *religieuses* of the order, and, for experience and competency, is entitled to public confidence not only in Canada but also throughout the United States.

STRANGERS ADMITTED TO VISIT.

ACADEMY

OF

JESUS-MARIE

HIGH above the umbrageous groves of SOUS-LES-BOIS for many years the attractive Villa of Errol Boyd Lindsay, Esq., looms out the majestic ACADEMY OF JESUS-MARIE, an institution for the education of young ladies. It is owned and conducted by the french nuns, of Jesus-Marie well known for the excellence of their teaching. The system followed in that convent is that of father Lacordaire, which is well suited to develope the reasoning and judgment of the pupils who are not required to learn anything by memory, but exclusively by analysis. All the subjects comprised in a classical course of studies, are taught in this convent.

As to sanitary arrangements, this Academy is one of the best institutions in Quebec. Ventilation and airing in every room is perfect and the place where the convent is situated is one of the healthiest around the City. The ground occupies an area of several acres and is ornamented with trees, walks and gardens, giving a rural appearance to the place and a great deal of comfort and amusement to the pupils.

This convent is about three miles from Quebec, on St Louis road, to the north of the parish church of St. Colomban of Sillery. It is a lofty white brick building, roomy and built with all the modern improvements, under the direction of Rev. Mr. Audette, member of the board of Arts and Manufactures. From the roof of the building, one may enjoy one of the grandest views of Quebec, the Plains of Abraham, the St. Lawrence and the surrounding country.

To Tourists, &c.

The undersigned, one of the oldest Publishers and Booksellers in the City, begs to call the attention of Tourists, Strangers and others, to his selection of Canadian works (English and French) for sale : he is now making a speciality of Guide-Books Histories of Canada, Sketches of Canadian Literature as well as standard French works, History, Novels, Science.

In order to afford additional facilities to Tourists, he will have constantly at their service, one or more experienced and well informed Guides, for those who desire to *do* the city and environs.

F. X. GARANT & CIE,
Fabrique street.

ST. LOUIS STREET

QUEBEC.

This Hotel which is unrivalled for Size, Style and Locality, in Quebec, is open through the year for pleasure and business travel.

It is eligibly situated in the vicinity of the most delightful and fashionable promenades, the Governor's Garden, the Citadel, the Esplanade, the Place d'Armes, and Durham Terrace, which furnish the splendid views and magnificent scenery for which Quebec is so justly celebrated, and which is unsurpassed in any part of the world.

The Proprietor, in returning thanks for the very liberal patronage he has hitherto enjoyed, informs the public that this Hotel has been enlarged and refitted and can now accommodate 500 visitors and assures them that nothing will be wanting on his part that will conduce to the comfort and enjoyment of his guests.

WILLIS RUSSELL,
Proprietor.

LEGER BROUSSEAU,

No. 9, RUE BUADE, H V., QUEBEC,

Importateur de Livres, Papeterie, Cire, Cierges, Vins, Liqueurs, Etc., Etc.

FOURNISSEUR DES FABRIQUES,

IMPRIMEUR ET EDITEUR-PROPRIÉTAIRE

DU

"COURRIER DU CANADA."

Librairie, imprimerie, Reliure et ouvrages de Fantaisie, etc., etc. Médailles à l'exposition de Dublin, 1865 et à l'exposition de Paris, 1867.

CHS. HOUGH & SON,

LIVERY STABLE KEEPER,

AND

CARRIAGE BUILDER,

103, ANN STREET,

QUEBEC.

JAMES McCONE,
WHOLESALE AND RETAIL
GROCER,
WINE & LIQUOR MERCHANT
No. 108, St. John Street (within),
QUEBEC.

Goods delivered all over the City Free.

P. E. DUGAL,
HATTER & FURRIER,
INDIAN CURIOSITIES,
At the Sign of the Tiger,
FABRIQUE STREET, UPPER TOWN,
QUEBEC.

OPPOSITE JESUITS BARRACKS.

F. X GARANT & CO.,

BOOKSELLERS

No. 6, Fabrique Street, Quebec, P. Q.

Next door to the Seminary.

Import from England, France, Germany, and of the Continent, goods, such as Books, Perfumeries, Church Ornements, Gold and Silver Lace, Gold and Silver Fringe ; Gold and Silver Tassels, etc ; Bells for Churches, Wax Candles, Wine for Mass, etc., etc.

— ALSO : —

Sherry, Brandy, Ginger Wine, Gin, Port Wine, Champagne, etc., all of first quality, and analysed by H. Larue Esq., M. D.

Always on hand, the collection of all the Canadian Works, such : Maple Leaves ; Album du Tourist, etc. by J. M. LeMoine ; History of Canada by Ferland ; History of Canada 2 vols., translated from Garneau by Bell ; works of H. Larue ; History of the Ursclines, 3 vols ; Canada under the Union 2 vols. etc., by Turcotte ; works of Father Tanguay ; works of P. Lemay ; works of Hon. P. Chauveau ; works of Faucher de St. Maurice, etc., etc.

OLIVIER MONTREUIL,

Carriages for Hire,

To be found at the steamboat landing

And at the Stand, Upper Town Market,

OR AT HIS RESIDENCE

No. 45½, D'AIGUILLON Street,

St. John's Suburb, QUEBEC.

Places of interest in and around the City of Quebec.

Durham Terrace.	English Cathedral.	the taking of Quebec.
Grand Battery.	Drive out St. Louis and	Falls of Montmorency
French Cathedral.	through St. Foy's road	and Natural Steps (13
Seminary Chapel.	Where Montgomery fell	miles drive.)
Governor's Garden.	Plains of Abraham	
Citadel.	where Wolfe fell at	

The above mentioned places are one day's drive.

Any persons wishing to visit other places the next day, will do well to agree with the driver before leaving as they will save money and time.

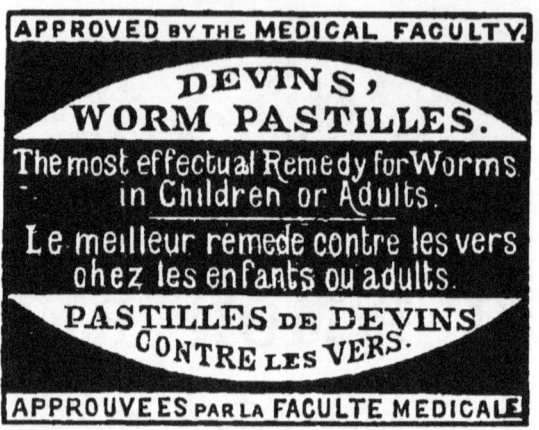

☞ For sale by all Druggists, also by Ed. Giroux & Brother, John S. Burke, W. H. LaRoche, Quebec, W. E. Brunet, J. J. Veldon, St. Roch.

DEVINS & BOLTON'S
PURE QUININE WINE,

Is the only wine which has received the sanction and approval of the Medical Faculty and by its unquestionable quality and its well known merits does not deceive the public.

It is specially recommended and adapted for children and delicate females, to mothers after confinement and to the weak or infirm whether from age or disease; is scientifically prepared with Howard's Sulphate of Quinine and fine grape wine, so as to possess the medicinal properties of this famous Tonic in a simple, pleasant and reliable form.

DIRECTIONS.—*From half to one wine glassfull, three times a day before meals.*

CAUTION.—See that you get DEVINS & BOLTON'S *PURE QUININE WINE.*

Sold by John Ross & Co., and Gibb, Laird & Co., Wholesale Grocers, G. & C. Hossack, T. Poston, Arthur Dion, and J. B. Z. Dubeau, Retail Grocers; also, by F. X. Garant & Co., Booksellers, Ed. Giroux & Brother, and John E. Burke, Chemist, Quebec.

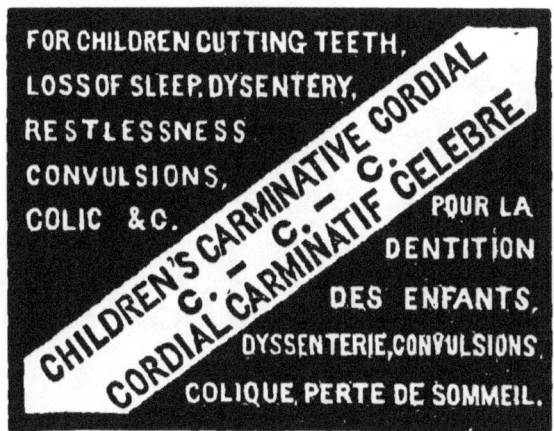

☞ For sale by all Druggists and by Ed. Giroux & Brother, John E. Burke and W. H. LaRoche, Quebec, W. E. Brunet, J. J. Veldon, St. Roch.

NO MORE GREY HAIRS
Lubin's Parisian Hair Renewer.

RESTORES GREY HAIR TO ITS ORIGINAL Color, Beauty and Softness; Keeps the Head Clean, Cool and free from Dandruff; Cures Irritations and Itching of the Scalp; gives a beautiful Gloss and Perfume to the Hair; will STOP ITS FALLING OUT in a few days; will not soil the skin or most delicate head dress; it gives entire satisfaction to those who use it, and is much cheaper than all other preparations, for when using it, you require neither Oil nor Pomatum.

In Large Sized Bottles only 50 Cents.

Principal Laboratory, No. 17, Rue Vivienne, Paris.

☞ For sale in Quebec at Ed. Giroux & Brother, John E. Burke, W. H. LaRoche, and W. E. Brunet, and J. J. Veldon, St. Roch.

ESTABLISHEE 1830

FISHER & BLOUIN,
(Late Jos. Auld),

MARKET PLACE,

Fabrique Street,
QUEBEC.

Keeps constantly on hands a large assortment in their line consisting of

Harness of all description,
LADIES & GENTLEMEN RIDING SADDLES,
Bridles, &c., English made.

— ALSO —

SOLID LEATHER TRUNKS,

AND

Portmanteaux, Valises, Coat Cases, and
BAGS OF ALL KINDS,
And all sorts of Fancy Work in RUSSIA and MORRACCO LEATHER, &c.

☞ All at the lowest possible price. ☜

D. MORGAN & SONS,

Tailors to His Excellency the Governor General,

MOUNTAIN HILL,
QUEBEC.
BRANCH HOUSE,
22, Sparks Street, OTTAWA.

G. & C. HOSSACK,

IMPORTERS OF
WINES, LIQUORS AND GENERAL GROCERIES,

The Freshest & Choicest Variety of Black Hamburg Grapes,

Chasselas Doré, Frontignan,

Royal Muscadine Grapes, in Season,

TO SPORTSMEN.
Outfits: potted Meats & Provisions,
CAREFULLY PACKED FOR SHIPMENT TO
SALMON RIVERS.

C. DARVEAU,
JOB PRINTER,
Copper Plate Printer & Stereotyper,
82, MOUNTAIN HILL, QUEBEC.

EN VENTE A

L'IMPRIMERIE C. DARVEAU,
82, Rue de la Montagne,
QUEBEC.

LES OUVRAGES SUIVANTS :

La Flore Canadienne, par l'abbé Provancher.......$2.00
Traité Elémentaire de Botanique, par le même.....$0.35
Le Verger, le Potager et le Parterre, par le même..$1.00
Œuvres Complètes de l'abbé Casgrain............$1.50
Manière d'élever les jeunes enfants, par le Dr. LaRue.$0.35

MÉLANGES ARCHÉOLOGIQUES

ET

BIOGRAPHIQUES

Rangés par ordre alphabétique pour l'usage et la commodité du Touriste par J. A. Malouin, avocat. auteur d'un calendrier perpétuel.

F. X. GARANT & CIE.,

ÉDITEURS.

1 volume grand in-8 vo., 500 pages, souscription $1.00, payable à la livraison de l'ouvrage.

On peut souscrire aussi chez Messrs. Rolland & Fils, Montréal,

chez tous les Libraires de Québec.

au " Journal des Trois-Rivières."

chez le Rev. Mr. Tanguay, Ottawa.

WORKS

PUBLISHED

BY J. M. LE MOINE.

ENGLISH.

LEGENDARY LORE OF THE LOWER ST. LAWRENCE, (1 vol. in-32)	1862
MAPLE LEAVES, (1st Series) (1 vol. in-8o)	1863
" " (2nd Series) (1 vol. in-8o)	1864
" " (3rd Series) (1 vol. in-8o)	1865
THE TOURIST'S NOTE BOOK, (1 vol. in-64) by Cosmopolite	1870
SWORD OF BRIGADIER GENERAL MONTGOMERY, (A Memoir) 1 vol. in-64)	1870
JOTTINGS FROM CANADIAN HISTORY, (Stewart's Quarterly)	1871
TRIFLES FROM MY PORT FOLIO, (New Dominion Monthly)	1872
MAPLE LEAVES, (New Series)	1873*
QUEBEC, PAST & PRESENT	1876
THE TOURIST'S NOTE BOOK (second edition)	1876

FRENCH.

L'ORNITHOLOGIE DU CANADA, (2 vol. in-8o)	1860
LES PECHERIES DU CANADA, (1 vol. in-8o)	1863
MEMOIRES DE MONTCALM VENGEE, (1 vol. in-32)	1865
L'ALBUM CANADIEN	1870
L'ALBUM DU TOURISTE, (1 vol. in-8o)	1873*

* For sale at Messrs. DAWSON & Co., Lower-Town, and at F. X. GARANT & Co., Fabrique Street, Quebec.

www.ingramcontent.com/pod-product-compliance
Lightning Source LLC
Chambersburg PA
CBHW020102170426
43199CB00009B/368